KEYBOARD SHORTCUTS

FOR MAC

2020 EDITION

JORDAN KENNEDY

Keyboard Shortcuts for Mac

ISBN (paperback): 978-0-578-70250-6
ISBN (ebook): 978-0-578-70252-0
July 2020, First Edition

Trademarks

Marked names, logos, and images may appear in this book. Rather than use a trademark symbol with every occurrence of a trademark name, logo, or image, we used the names, logos, and images only in an editorial fashion and to benefit the trademark owner, with no intention of infringement of the trademark.

The use in this publication of trade names, trademarks, surface marks, and similar items, even if they are not identified as such, is not to be taken as an expression of opinion as to whether or not they are subject to the proprietary rights.

Warning and Disclaimer

Every effort has been made to make this book as complete and accurate as possible, but no warranty is implied. The information provided is on an "as is" basis. The author and publisher shall have neither liability nor responsibility to any person or entity with respect to a loss or damages arising from the information contained in this book.

Table of Contents

Professional Apps

Utility Apps

*To my mother,
who encouraged my
computer nerdery
to flourish*

Keyboard Symbols Explained

Welcome to *Keyboard Shortcuts for Mac*. This book is a reference guide to keyboard shortcuts and will help you become a more productive Mac power user. This edition covers the macOS 10.15 Catalina operating system and related apps.

This guide will be referencing a standard Macintosh keyboard layout. Nearly all keyboard shortcuts you'll find in this book can be used with a standard keyboard for Mac (with or without TouchBar). Some apps use the additional keys found on an extended keyboard for Mac.

Symbol	Description
&	Ampersand
'	Apostrophe
←→↑↓	Arrow Keys
*	Asterisk
@	At Sign
\	Backslash
⇪	Caps Lock
^	Caret
:	Colon
,	Comma
⌘	Command
⌃	Control
⌫	Delete
$	Dollar Sign
↘	End
⏶	Enter
=	Equal Sign

Symbol	Description
↺	Escape
!	Exclamation Mark
⌦	Forward Delete
/	Forward Slash
fn	Function
`	Grave Accent
↖	Home
–	Hyphen / Minus Sign
<	Left Angle Bracket
[	Left Bracket
{	Left Curly Bracket
(	Left Parenthesis
#	Octothorpe / Pound
⌥	Option
⇟	Page Down
⇞	Page Up
%	Percent

Symbol	Description
.	Period
+	Plus Sign
?	Question Mark
"	Quotation Mark
↩	Return
>	Right Angle Bracket
]	Right Bracket
}	Right Curly Bracket
)	Right Parenthesis
;	Semicolon
⇧	Shift
␣	Space Bar
⇥	Tab
~	Tilde
_	Underscore
|	Vertical Bar

Startup

There are many tools and system features you can use upon startup by pressing and holding down certain key commands immediately after pressing the power button. If the keyboard shortcuts below don't work as described, be sure your wireless keyboard is plugged in. Many of these keyboard shortcuts will not work if your Mac has a firmware password enabled.

Keyboard Shortcut	Action
D	Start up to the diagnostic utility
Option-D	Start up to the diagnostic utility over the Internet
N	Start up from a NetBoot server
Option-N	Start up from a NetBoot server defaults
T	Start up in target disk mode
Shift	Start up in safe mode
Option	Shows the Startup Manager which allows you to choose from any bootable medium
Command-R	Start up from the built-in macOS Recovery system
Command-Option-R	Start up from macOS Recovery over the Internet with the latest operating system that is compatible with your Mac
Command-Option-P-R	Resets the PRAM or NVRAM
Command-S	Start up in single-user mode
Command-V	Start up in verbose mode
Eject F12	Eject optical disks

General

Throughout this book, you'll notice a pattern of generally accepted keyboard shortcuts that work just about anywhere. For example, nearly all apps use the same keyboard shortcut for cut, copy, and paste. This chapter is a collection of commonly used keyboard shortcuts that can generally be used system wide.

Keyboard Shortcut	Action
Command-X	Cut the selected text or item and copy it to the clipboard
Command-C	Copy the selected text or item to the clipboard
Command-V	Paste the contents of the clipboard
Command-Z	Undo the previous command
Command-Shift-Z	Redo, revoking the undo command
Command-A	Select all items
Command-F	Find items in a document
Command-G	Find again: find the next occurrence of the item already found
Command-Shift-G	Find the previous occurrence
Command-H	Hide the windows of the frontmost app
Command-Option-H	View the front app but hide all other apps
Command-M	Minimize the front window to the Dock
Command-Option-M	Minimize all windows of the frontmost app to the Dock
Command-O	Open the selected item or open a dialog to select a file to open
Command-P	Print the document
Command-S	Save the document
Command-T	Open a new tab
Command-W	Close the frontmost window

 DID YOU KNOW?
Many, if not all, keyboard shortcuts can be found in the app's menu items.

Keyboard Shortcut	Action
Command-Option-W	Close all windows of the app
Command-Option-Escape	Force quit an app
Command-Space Bar	Show or hide the Spotlight search field
Command-Option-Space Bar	Perform a Spotlight search from a Finder window
Command-Control-Space Bar	Show the Character Viewer, which you can choose emoji and other symbols
Command-Control-F	Use the app in full screen
Space Bar	Use Quick Look to preview a selected item
Command-Tab	Switch to the next most recently used app among your open apps
Command-Shift-3	Take a screenshot of your whole desktop screen(s)
Command-Shift-4	Allows you to select an area of the screen to capture
Command-Shift-4-Space Bar	Allows you to take screenshots of windows or menus
Command-Shift-5	Take a screenshot or make a screen recording with additional options
Command-Comma	Open preferences for the frontmost app
Power Button	Press to turn on your Mac or wake it from sleep Continue holding to force your Mac to turn off
Command-Option-Power Button Command-Option-Eject	Put your Mac to sleep
Control-Shift-Power Button Control-Shift-Eject	Put your display(s) to sleep
Control-Power Button Control-Eject	Display a dialog asking whether you want to restart, sleep, or shut down
Command-Control-Power Button	Force your Mac to restart, without prompting to save any open and unsaved documents
Command-Control-Eject	Restart your Mac
Command-Option-Control-Power Button Command-Option-Control-Eject	Quit all apps, then shut down your Mac. If any open documents have unsaved changes, you will be asked whether you want to save them.
Command-Control-Q	Immediately lock your screen
Command-Shift-Q	Log out of your macOS user account
Command-Option-Shift-Q	Log out immediately without confirming

Finder

Every time you use your Macintosh, this happy-faced app is there to help you navigate files and keep them organized.

Keyboard Shortcut	Action
Command-D	Duplicate the selected files
Command-E	Eject the selected disk or volume
Command-F	Start a Spotlight search in the Finder window
Command-I	Show the Get Info window for a selected file
Command-R	Show the original file for the selected alias
Command-Shift-C	Open the Computer window
Command-Shift-D	Open the Desktop folder
Command-Shift-F	Open the Recents window
Command-Shift-G	Open a Go to Folder window
Command-Shift-H	Open the Home folder
Command-Shift-I	Open iCloud Drive
Command-Shift-K	Open the Network window
Command-Option-L	Open the Downloads folder
Command-Shift-N	Create a new folder
Command-Shift-O	Open the Documents folder
Command-Shift-P	Show or hide the Preview pane in Finder windows
Command-Shift-R	Open the AirDrop window
Command-Shift-T	Show or hide the tab bar in Finder windows
Command-Control-Shift-T	Add selected Finder item to the Dock
Command-Shift-U	Open the Utilities folder
Command-Option-D	Show or hide the Dock
Command-Control-T	Add the selected item to the sidebar

Keyboard Shortcut	Action
Command-Option-P	Hide or show the path bar in Finder windows
Command-Option-S	Hide or show the Sidebar in Finder windows
Command-Forward Slash	Hide or show the status bar in Finder windows
Command-J	Show view options
Command-K	Open the Connect to Server window
Command-L	Make an alias of the selected item
Command-N	Open a new Finder window
Command-Option-N	Create a new Smart Folder
Command-T	Show or hide the tab bar when a single tab is open in the Finder window
Command-Option-T	Show or hide the toolbar when a single tab is open in the Finder window
Command-Option-V	Move files in the clipboard from original location to the current location
Command-Y	Use Quick Look to preview the selected files
Command-Option-Y	View a Quick Look slideshow of the selected files
Command-1	Show items in the Finder window as icons
Command-2	Show items in the Finder window as a list
Command-3	Show items in the Finder window in columns
Command-4	Show items in the Finder window in a gallery
Command-Left Bracket	Go to the previous folder
Command-Right Bracket	Go to the next folder
Command-Up Arrow	Open the folder that contains the current folder
Command-Control-Up Arrow	Open the folder that contains the current folder in a new window
Command-Down Arrow	Open the selected item
Right Arrow	Open the selected folder while in list view
Left Arrow	Close the selected folder while in list view
Command-Delete	Move the selected item to the Trash
Command-Shift-Delete	Empty the Trash
Command-Option-Shift-Delete	Empty the Trash without confirmation dialog
Command-Brightness Up	Turn target display mode on or off
Command-Brightness Down	Turn video mirroring on or off when connected to multiple displays
Option-Brightness Up/Down	Open Displays preferences
Control-Brightness Up/Down	Change the brightness of your external display, if supported

Keyboard Shortcut	Action
Option-Shift-Brightness Up/Down	Adjust the display brightness in smaller increments
Option-Mission Control	Open Mission Control preferences
Command-Mission Control	Show the desktop
Control-Down Arrow	Show all windows of the front app
Option-Volume Up	Open Sound preferences This works with any of the volume keys
Option-Shift-Volume Up/Down	Adjust the sound volume in smaller steps
Option-Keyboard Brightness Up/Down	Open Keyboard preferences
Option-Shift-Keyboard Brightness Up/Down	Adjust the keyboard brightness in smaller steps
Option Key While Double-Clicking	Open the item in a separate window, then close the original window
Command Key While Double-Clicking	Open a folder in a separate tab or window
Command Key While Dragging to Another Volume	Move the dragged item to the other volume, instead of copying it
Option Key While Dragging	Copy the dragged item
Command-Option While Dragging	Make an alias of the dragged item
Option-Click a Disclosure Triangle	Open all folders within the selected folder when in list view
Command Click a Window Title	See the folders that contain the current folder

Documents

The ability to create and edit documents is crucial to productivity and exists in a ton of apps. From replying to an email to writing a proposal in Pages, there is a wide variety of keyboard shortcuts to aid you in managing your document.

Keyboard Shortcut	Action
Command-B	Boldface the selected text, or toggle boldfacing on or off
Command-I	Italicize the selected text, or toggle italics on or off
Command-K	Add a web link
Command-U	Underline the selected text or toggle underlining on or off
Command-T	Show or hide the Fonts window
Command-D	Select the Desktop folder from within an Open dialog or Save dialog
Command-Control-D	Show or hide the definition of the selected word
Command-Shift-Colon	Display the Spelling and grammar window
Command-Semicolon	Find misspelled words in the document
Option-Delete	Delete the word to the left of the insertion point
Control-H	Delete the character to the left of the insertion point. Or use Delete.
Control-D	Delete the character to the right of the insertion point. Or use Function-Delete.
Function-Delete	Forward delete on keyboards that don't have a Forward Delete key
Control-K	Delete the text between the insertion point and the end of the line or paragraph
Function-Up Arrow Page Up	Scroll up one page
Function-Down Arrow Page Down	Scroll down one page
Function-Left Arrow Home Key	Scroll to the beginning of a document
Function-Right Arrow End Key	Scroll to the end of a document

Keyboard Shortcut	Action
Command-Up Arrow	Move the insertion point to the beginning of the document
Command-Down Arrow	Move the insertion point to the end of the document
Command-Left Arrow	Move the insertion point to the beginning of the current line
Command-Right Arrow	Move the insertion point to the end of the current line
Option-Left Arrow	Move the insertion point to the beginning of the previous word
Option-Right Arrow	Move the insertion point to the end of the next word
Command-Shift-Up Arrow	Select the text between the insertion point and the beginning of the document
Command-Shift-Down Arrow	Select the text between the insertion point and the end of the document
Command-Shift-Left Arrow	Select the text between the insertion point and the beginning of the current line
Command-Shift-Right Arrow	Select the text between the insertion point and the end of the current line
Shift-Up Arrow	Extend text selection to the nearest character at the same horizontal location on the line above
Shift-Down Arrow	Extend text selection to the nearest character at the same horizontal location on the line below
Shift-Left Arrow	Extend text selection one character to the left
Shift-Right Arrow	Extend text selection one character to the right
Option-Shift-Up Arrow	Extend text selection to the beginning of the current paragraph, then to the beginning of the following paragraph if pressed again
Option-Shift-Down Arrow	Extend text selection to the end of the current paragraph, then to the end of the following paragraph if pressed again
Option-Shift-Left Arrow	Extend text selection to the beginning of the current word, then to the beginning of the following word if pressed again
Option-Shift-Right Arrow	Extend text selection to the end of the current word, then to the end of the following word if pressed again
Control-A	Move to the beginning of the line or paragraph
Control-E	Move to the end of a line or paragraph
Control-F	Move one character forward
Control-B	Move one character backward
Control-L	Center the cursor or selection in the visible area
Control-P	Move up one line
Control-N	Move down one line
Control-O	Insert a new line after the insertion point

Keyboard Shortcut	Action
Control-T	Swap the character behind the insertion point with the character in front of the insertion point
Command-Left Curly Bracket	Left align the text
Command-Right Curly Bracket	Right align the text
Command-Shift-Vertical Bar	Center align the text
Command-Option-F	Go to the search field
Command-Option-T	Show or hide a toolbar in the app
Command-Option-C	Copy Style Copy the formatting settings of the selected item to the clipboard
Command-Option-V	Paste Style Apply the copied style to the selected item
Command-Option-Shift-V	Paste and Match Style Apply the style of the surrounding content to the item pasted within that content
Command-Option-I	Show or hide the inspector window
Command-Shift-P	Show page setup for printing
Command-Shift-S	Display the Save As dialog, or duplicate the current document
Command-Shift-Minus Sign	Decrease the size of the selected item
Command-Shift-Plus Sign	Increase the size of the selected item. Command-Equal Sign performs the same function.
Command-Shift-Question mark	Open the Help menu

Accessibility

One of the greatest features of any modern Mac is the powerful accessibility features to control and manage your computer with a keyboard or other assistive device.

Keyboard Shortcut	Action
Command-Option-F5	Display Accessibility Options
Command-F5	Turn VoiceOver on or off
Option-Control-F8	Open VoiceOver Utility, if VoiceOver is turned on
Command-Option-8	Turn zoom on or off
Command-Option-Plus Sign	Zoom in
Command-Option-Minus Sign	Zoom out
Command-Option-Control-8	Invert colors
Command-Option-Control-Comma	Reduce contrast
Command-Option-Control-Period	Increase contrast
Control-F7 Function-Control-F7	Switch between navigation of all controls on the screen, or only text boxes and lists
Tab	Move to the next control
Shift-Tab	Move to the previous control
Control-Tab	Move to the next control when a text field is selected
Control-Shift-Tab	Move the focus to the previous grouping of controls
Arrow keys	Move to the adjacent item in a list, tab group, or menu Move sliders and adjusters (Up Arrow to increase values, Down Arrow to decrease values)
Control-Arrow keys	Move to a control adjacent to the text field
Space Bar	Choose the selected menu item
Return Enter	Click the default button or perform the default action
Escape	Click the Cancel button or close a menu without choosing an item
Control-Shift-F6	Move the focus to the previous panel

Keyboard Shortcut	Action
Control-F8 Function-Control-F8	Move to the status menu in the menu bar
Command-Grave Accent	Activate the next open window in the front app
Command-Shift-Grave Accent	Activate the previous open window in the front app
Command-Option-Grave accent	Move the focus to the window drawer
Left Arrow Right Arrow	Move from menu to menu
Return	Open a selected menu
Up Arrow Down Arrow	Move to menu items in the selected menu
Type the menu item's name	Jump to a menu item in the selected menu
Return	Choose the selected menu item
8 Numeric Keypad 8	Move up
K Numeric Keypad 2	Move down
U Numeric Keypad4	Move left
O Numeric Keypad 6	Move right
J Numeric Keypad 1	Move diagonally down and to the left
L Numeric Keypad 3	Move diagonally down and to the right
7 Numeric Keypad 7	Move diagonally up and to the left
9 Numeric Keypad 9	Move diagonally up and to the right
I Numeric Keypad 5	Press the mouse button
M Numeric Keypad 0	Hold the mouse button
Period	Release the mouse button

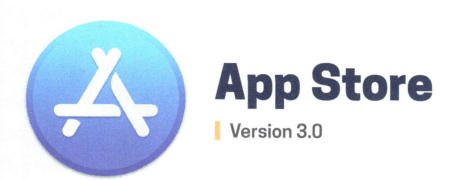

App Store

Version 3.0

Keyboard Shortcut	Action
Command-1	Show Discover apps
Command-2	Show Arcade apps
Command-3	Show Create apps
Command-4	Show Work apps
Command-5	Show Play apps
Command-6	Show Develop apps
Command-7	Show Categories apps
Command-8	Show Updates
Command-F	Search for an app
Command-R	Refresh the current page
Command-Left Bracket	Go to the previous page

Automator

| Version 2.10

Keyboard Shortcut	Action
Option-Click the disclosure triangle in the title bar of one of the actions	Collapse all the actions in a workflow
Command-H	Hide this app
Command-Option-H	Hide all other apps
Command-N	Create a new workflow
Command-O	Open a dialog to select a file to open
Command-W	Close the frontmost window
Command-S	Save the document
Command-Shift-S	Duplicate the document
Command-Option-Shift-C	Convert the document
Command-Shift-P	Show page setup for printing
Command-P	Print the document
Command-Z	Undo the previous command
Command-Shift-Z	Redo, revoking the undo command
Command-X	Cut the selected text or item and copy it to the clipboard
Command-C	Copy the selected text or item to the clipboard
Command-V	Paste the contents of the clipboard
Command-A	Select all items
Command-D	Duplicate the selected item
Command-Option-F	Find action (sets the prompt to the search field)
Command-F	Find items in a document or app
Command-G	Find again: find the next occurrence of the item already found

Keyboard Shortcut	Action
Command-Shift-G	Find the previous occurrence
Command-Colon	Show spelling and grammar
Command-Semicolon	Check spelling
Command-Option-T	Open special characters window
Command-Option-L	Show the log
Command-R	Run workflow or action
Command-Period	Stop workflow or action
Command-Option-R	Record the workflow
Command-K	Show results
Command-Up Arrow	Move up in the document
Command-Down Arrow	Move down in the document
Command-Shift-J	Show in Library
Command-M	Minimize the frontmost window to the Dock

Books

Version 2.4

Keyboard Shortcut	Action
Command-N	Add a new collection to your library
Command-Shift-O	Add books to your library
Command-D	Bookmark the page you're currently viewing
Command-F	Open a book's search field after opening the search field, just start typing, then press Return to search
Command-T	Show a book's table of contents
Command-Shift-T	Show a book's thumbnails
Command-3	Show your notes in the book's margins
Command-4	Show all notes and highlights in the Notes panel
Command-5	Show study cards for a book
Command-6	Show a book's glossary
Command-1	See one page at a time
Command-2	See two pages at a time
Command-0	See the book at its actual size
Command-Plus Sign	Zoom in to a book
Command-Minus Sign	Zoom out of a book
Command-Control-F	Switch to full-screen view
Right Arrow Down Arrow Page Down	Go to the next page, or the next image, call-out, or question in expanded interactive media
Left Arrow Up Arrow Page Up	Go to the previous page, or the previous image, call-out, or question in expanded interactive media
Command-Shift-Right Arrow	Go to the next chapter

Keyboard Shortcut	Action
Command-Shift-Left Arrow	Go to the previous chapter
Command-Left Bracket	Go back to your previous spot in the book
Command-Right Bracket	Go forward to your original spot in the book
Command-Shift-B	Open the Book Store
Command-Shift-A	Open the Audiobook Store
Command-L	Open your library

Calculator

Version 10.15

Keyboard Shortcut	Action
Escape C Clear	Clear
Option-Escape	Clear all
Option-Minus Sign	Negate the displayed value
Percent Sign	Percent
Forward Slash	Divide
Asterisk	Multiply
Minus Sign	Subtract
Plus Sign	Add
Equal Sign	Equal
Delete key	Remove the most recently entered digit or letter
Caret	Raise the displayed value to the power of the next value entered
E	Calculate the natural logarithm of the displayed value
Exclamation Point	Calculate the factorial of the displayed value
Shift-E	Exponential notation
Command-E	Swap the bottom two numbers on the stack
Command-Up Arrow	Move the most recently entered number up on the stack
Command-Down Arrow	Move the most recently entered number down on the stack
Command-Delete	Remove the bottom number from the stack
Command-H	Hide this app
Command-Option-H	Hide all other apps
Command-Q	Quit this app

Keyboard Shortcut	Action
Command-W	Close the frontmost window
Command-Shift-S	Open the Save As dialog for the paper tape
Command-Shift-P	Page setup for printing
Command-P	Print the paper tape
Command-Z	Undo the previous command
Command-Shift-Z	Redo, revoking the undo command
Command-X	Cut the selected text or item and copy it to the clipboard
Command-C	Copy the selected text or item to the clipboard
Command-V	Paste the contents of the clipboard
Command-A	Select all items
Press Function Twice	Start voice dictation
Command-Control-Space Bar	Show the Character Viewer, which you can choose emoji and other symbols
Command-1	Show the basic calculator
Command-2	Show the scientific calculator
Command-3	Show the programmer calculator
Command-R	Display RPN mode
Command-M	Minimize the frontmost window to the Dock
Command-T	Show the paper tape

Calendar

Version 11

Keyboard Shortcut	Action
Command-Right Arrow	Go to the next day, week, month, or year
Command-Left Arrow	Go to the previous day, week, month, or year
Command-T	Go to today's date
Command-Shift-T	Go to a specific date
Command-1	Switch to Day view
Command-2	Switch to Week view
Command-3	Switch to Month view
Command-4	Switch to Year view
Command-Control-F	Switch to full-screen view
Escape	Exit full-screen view
Command-Plus Sign	Make text bigger
Command-Minus Sign	Make text smaller
Command-R	Refresh all calendars
Space Bar (with the Calendar list open)	Select or deselect the checkbox next to the selected calendar
Command-Click any calendar's checkbox	Select or deselect all the checkboxes next to calendars in the Calendar list
Command-Option-Click any calendar's checkbox	Select the checkbox next to the selected calendar and deselect all other checkboxes
Command-Shift-N	Add a new calendar group
Command-Option-S	Add a new subscribed calendar
Command-P	Print a day, week, month, or year calendar
Command-N	Add a new event
Command-E	Edit the selected event

Keyboard Shortcut	Action
Command-Option-I	Edit the selected event in the inspector window
Tab (while an event is open)	Go to the next field
Shift-Tab (while an event is open)	Go to the previous field
Return (while an event is open) Escape (while an event is open)	Close the event editor
Tab	Select the next event
Shift-Tab	Select the previous event
Arrow keys	Select the next or previous event
Command-F	Search for events
Control-Click the event, then choose a calendar from the shortcut menu	Move an event to another calendar
Option-Control-Up Arrow	Move the selected event 15 minutes earlier (in Day or Week view); move the selected event one week earlier (in Month view)
Option-Control-Down Arrow	Move the selected event 15 minutes later (in Day or Week view); move the selected event one week later (in Month view)
Option-Control-Right Arrow	Move the selected event one day later (in Week or Month view); move the selected event one week later (in Month view)
Option-Control-Left Arrow	Move the selected event one day earlier (in Week or Month view); move the selected event one week earlier (in Month view)
Command-I	Show information for a calendar or event
Command-P	Print the selected events or events in a time range
Command-Shift-A	Show or hide the Availability panel
Command-Comma	Open the preferences window

Chess

Version 3.17

Keyboard Shortcut	Action
Command-Comma	Open the preferences window
Command-H	Hide this app
Command-Option-H	Hide all other apps
Command-Q	Quit this app
Command-N	Create a new game
Command-O	Open a game
Command-W	Close the frontmost window
Command-S	Save the chess game
Command-Shift-S	Duplicate the chess game
Command-Z	Undo the previous command
Command-Shift-Z	Redo, revoking the undo command
Command-X	Cut the selected text or item and copy it to the clipboard
Command-C	Copy the selected text or item to the clipboard
Command-V	Paste the contents of the clipboard
Press Function Twice	Start voice dictation
Command-Control-Space Bar	Show the Character Viewer, which you can choose emoji and other symbols
Command-Right Bracket	Show a hint
Command-Left Bracket	Show the last move
Command-L	Show the game log
Command-W	Close the frontmost window
Command-M	Minimize the frontmost window to the Dock
Command-Control-F	Enter full screen

Contacts

▍ Version 12.0

Keyboard Shortcut	Action
Command-Comma	Open the preferences window
Command-N	Create a card for a new contact
Command-Shift-N	Create a new group (or folder, if you use an Exchange account in Contacts)
Command-Option-N	Create a new Smart Group
Command-S	Save changes
Command-O	Import contacts from other apps
Command-P	Print mailing labels, envelopes, and contact lists in Contacts on Mac
Command-L	Edit the current contact
Command-1	Show or hide groups
Command-2	View a list and a card
Command-Option-L	Show or hide the last import
Command-Right Bracket	Go to the next card
Command-Left Bracket	Go to the previous card
Command-Shift-L	Merge selected cards (that are in the same account) or link selected cards (that are in different accounts)
Command-Backslash	Mark a card as a company or a person
Command-Option-I	Choose a custom image for a contact
Command-I	Open a card in a new window

Dictionary

Version 2.3.0

Keyboard Shortcut	Action
Command-Comma	Open the preferences window
Command-H	Hide this app
Command-Option-H	Hide all other apps
Command-Q	Quit this app
Command-N	Open a new Dictionary window
Command-T	Open a new tab
Command-W	Close the frontmost window
Command-P	Print the document
Command-Z	Undo the previous command
Command-Shift-Z	Redo, revoking the undo command
Command-X	Cut the selected text or item and copy it to the clipboard
Command-C	Copy the selected text or item to the clipboard
Command-V	Paste the contents of the clipboard
Command-A	Select all items
Command-Option-F	Search for a new word
Command-F	Find items in a document or app
Command-G	Find again: find the next occurrence of the item already found
Command-Shift-G	Find the previous occurrence
Command-E	Use selection for find
Command-J	Jump to selection
Command-Left Bracket	Go to previous selection
Command-Right Bracket	Go to next selection

Keyboard Shortcut	Action
Command-0	Show all dictionaries
Command-1	Show the New Oxford American Dictionary
Command-2	Show the Oxford American Writer's Thesaurus
Command-3	Show the Apple Dictionary
Command-4	Show Wikipedia
Command-Right Curly Bracket	Select the next dictionary
Command-Left Curly Bracket	Select the previous dictionary
Command-M	Minimize the frontmost window to the Dock
Control-Shift-Tab	Show the previous tab
Control-Tab	Show the next tab
Command-Shift-Backslash	Show all tabs

FaceTime

Version 5.0

Keyboard Shortcut	Action
Command-Comma	Open the preferences window
Command-H	Hide this app
Command-Option-H	Hide all other apps
Command-K	Turn FaceTime off
Command-Q	Quit this app
Command-W	Close the frontmost window
Command-M	Minimize the frontmost window to the Dock
Command-Control-F	Enter or exit full-screen view during a video call
Command-R	Use landscape or portrait during a video call

Find My

Version 1.0

Keyboard Shortcut	Action
Command-1	Switch to the People list
Command-2	Switch to the Devices list
Up Arrow Down Arrow	Within the list of people or devices, move up or down
Command-Shift-L	Share my location
Command-H	Hide this app
Command-Option-H	Hide all other apps
Command-Q	Quit this app
Command-W	Close the frontmost window
Command-M	Minimize the frontmost window to the Dock
Command-Control-F	Enter or exit full-screen view
Command-Plus Sign	Zoom in
Command-Minus Sign	Zoom out

Font Book

| Version 10.0

Keyboard Shortcut	Action
Command-Comma	Open the preferences window
Command-H	Hide this app
Command-Option-H	Hide all other apps
Command-Q	Quit this app
Command-N	Create a new collection
Command-Option-N	Create a new library
Command-O	Add fonts
Command-W	Close the frontmost window
Command-S	Save report
Command-R	Show in finder
Command-P	Print the document
Command-Z	Undo the previous command
Command-Shift-Z	Redo, revoking the undo command
Command-X	Cut the selected text or item and copy it to the clipboard
Command-C	Copy the selected text or item to the clipboard
Command-V	Paste the contents of the clipboard
Command-Delete	Delete the selected item
Command-A	Select all items
Command-Shift-D	Disable selected font family
Command-Shift-E	Disable the collection
Command-L	Look for enabled duplicates
Command-Option-F	Search for a font

Keyboard Shortcut	Action
Command-F	Find items in a document or app
Command-G	Find again: find the next occurrence of the item already found
Command-Shift-G	Find the previous occurrence
Command-E	Use selection for find
Command-J	Jump to selection
Press Function Twice	Start voice dictation
Command-Control-Space Bar	Show the Character Viewer, which you can choose emoji and other symbols
Command-1	Show a sample of text for the selected font
Command-2	Show the repertoire of the selected font
Command-3	Set you own custom text of the selected font
Command-I	Show the font information
Command-Option-L	Hide/Show the sidebar
Command-Option-I	Hide/Show the preview pane
Command-Control-F	Enter full screen
Command-M	Minimize the frontmost window to the Dock

GarageBand

Version 10.3

Keyboard Shortcut	Action
R	Start recording
Enter (on numeric keypad)	Start playback
Zero (on numeric keypad)	Stop playback
Space Bar	Start or stop playback
Comma	Move the playhead back one bar
Period	Move the playhead forward one bar
Shift-Space Bar	Start playback from selection
Command-Shift-Period	Move the cycle range forward by one cycle length
Command-Shift-Comma	Move the cycle range backward by one cycle length
Function-Left Arrow Control-Home	Go to the beginning of selection
Option-Return	Go to the end of the last region
Return	Go to beginning
C	Turn the cycle area on or off
Command-Option-Control-S	Turn solo on or off for all soloed tracks
K	Turn the metronome on or off
Shift-K	Turn count-in on or off
Command-Comma	Open the preferences window
Command-K	Show or hide the Musical Typing window
B	Show or hide the Smart Controls window
N	Show or hide the Score Editor
P	Show or hide the Piano Roll Editor

Keyboard Shortcut	Action
O	Show or hide the Loop Browser
Y	Show or hide the Library
Shift-Backslash	Show or hide Quick Help
Command-Backslash	Show detailed help (if available)
Command-Control-F	Enter or exit Full Screen mode
Command-Option-O	Open the Movie window
Command-W	Close the frontmost window
Up Arrow	Select the next higher track
Down Arrow	Select the next lower track
Command-H	Hide this app
Command-Option-H	Hide other apps
Command-Q	Quit this app
Command-N	Create a new project
Command-O	Open an existing project
Command-S	Save the current project
Command-Shift-S	Save the current project by specifying the name and location
Tab	Change focus to next area in GarageBand window
Shift-Tab	Change focus to previous area in GarageBand window
Command-M	Minimize the frontmost window to the Dock
Command-Option-M	Minimize all other app windows
Right Bracket	Next Patch, Effect, or Instrument setting
Left Bracket	Previous Patch, Effect, or Instrument setting
M	Mute or unmute the selected track
S	Solo or unsolo the selected track
Control-I	Turn monitoring for the selected track on or off
Command-Z	Undo the previous command
Command-Shift-Z	Redo, revoking the undo command
Command-X	Cut the selected text or item and copy it to the clipboard
Command-C	Copy the selected text or item to the clipboard
Command-V	Paste the contents of the clipboard
Delete	Delete selected item

Keyboard Shortcut	Action
Command-A	Select all items
Command-Left Arrow	Horizontal zoom out
Command-Right Arrow	Horizontal zoom in
Function-Up Arrow Page Up	Page Up
Function-Down Arrow Page Down	Page Down
Function-Left Arrow Home	Page Left
Function-Right Arrow End	Page Right
A	Show or hide Automation lanes
Command-Option-N	Create a new track
Command-Option-A	Create a new audio track
Command-Option-S	Create a new software instrument track
Command-Option-U	Create a new Drummer track
Command-Delete	Delete the selected track
Left Arrow	Select the previous region on the selected track or event in the editor
Right Arrow	Select the next region on the selected track or event in the editor
L	Loop the selected region continuously
Q	Quantize selected events
Command-Option-Q	Undo Quantization
Command-Shift-V	Paste and replace the current selection
Command-J	Join regions or notes
Command-T	Split the selected region or event at the playhead position
Command-G	Turn Snap to Grid on or off
Command-Control-Shift-Delete	Delete all automation on the selected track
Control-R	Turn Record Enable for the selected track on or off
Command-Option-Delete	Cut the selected Arrangement Marker into sections
Shift-Return	Rename the selected track
Control-Shift-O	Add selected region to the Apple Loops Library
Shift-N	Rename the selected regions
Option-T	Configure the Track Header

Keyboard Shortcut	Action
E	Show or hide the Editor pane
Command-Option-P	Show or hide the note pad
F	Show or hide the Browsers pane
Command-Shift-M	Show or hide the master track
Command-Option-G	Show or hide the alignment guides
Option-Space Bar	Preview the selected audio (audio editor only)
Option-Up Arrow	Transpose selected notes up one semitone (Piano Roll and Score Editors only)
Option-Down Arrow	Transpose selected notes down one semitone (Piano Roll and Score Editors only)
Option-Shift-Up Arrow	Transpose selected notes up one octave (Piano Roll and Score Editors only)
Option-Shift-Down Arrow	Transpose selected notes down one octave (Piano Roll and Score Editors only)
Command-Shift-A	Show or hide the Arrangement track
Command-Shift-O	Show or hide the Movie track
Command-Shift-X	Show or hide the Transposition track
Command-Shift-T	Show or hide the Tempo track

Home

Version 4.0

Keyboard Shortcut	Action
Command-Shift-H	Edit Home
Command-Shift-R	Edit Room
Command-1	View the Home tab
Command-2	View the Rooms tab
Command-3	View the Automation tab

iMovie

Version 10.1.14

Keyboard Shortcut	Action
Command-Shift-Question Mark	Open the iMovie Help menu
Command-I	Import media
Space Bar	Play video beginning from the frame beneath the playhead or skimmer
Forward Slash	Play the selection
Backslash	Play the selected event, clip, or project from the beginning
Right Arrow	Move the playhead one frame forward
Left Arrow	Move the playhead one frame backward
Down Arrow	When playing a clip in the browser, jump forward to the next clip
Up Arrow	When playing a clip in the timeline, jump to the beginning of the current clip, or jump to the previous clip if the playhead is near the beginning of the current clip
Command-Shift-F	Play the selected item full screen
Escape	Exit full-screen view
Command-L	Loop playback
Control-Y	Show or hide clip information when skimming in the browser
Command-N	Create a new movie project
Command-Delete	Moves the selected clip, movie, trailer, or event to the Trash. If only part of a clip is selected, the entire clip is moved to the Trash.
Command-Comma	Open the preferences window
Command-A	Select all clips. To select all clips in the timeline, first click anywhere in the timeline. To select all clips in the browser, first click anywhere in the browser.
X	Select an entire clip
Hold down the R key and drag	Select part of a clip

Keyboard Shortcut	Action
Command-Shift-A	Deselect all clips
E	Add the selection to the movie
Q	Connect the selection to the clip at the playhead position
W	Insert the selection in the movie at the playhead position
Command-Shift-E	Automatically improve the video and audio quality of the selected clip
Command-X	Cut the selected frames
Command-C	Copy the selected frames
Command-Forward Slash	Paste the selected frames
Option-Forward Slash	Trim a clip in the timeline to the selected range
Command-B	Divide a clip at the playhead position
Option-Shift-R	Reset speed adjustments
Command-Option-V	Paste all adjustments
Command-Option-C	Paste color correction adjustments
Command-Option-R	Paste crop adjustments
Command-Option-A	Paste volume adjustments
Command-Option-L	Paste the video effect
Command-Option-O	Paste the audio effect
Command-Option-S	Paste speed adjustments
Command-Option-U	Paste video overlay settings. Pastes adjustments, depending on which type of video is selected.
Command-Option-M	Paste the map style
F	Rate the selection as favorite
U	Unmark selected frames
Delete key	Rate the selection as rejected, or delete the selection from the timeline
Command-Backslash	Open or close the clip trimmer when a clip is selected
Command-Forward Slash	Open or close the precision editor
V	Open voiceover controls in the viewer
Shift-S	Turn on or silence audio while skimming video
Command-Shift-M	Mute audio in a clip
Command-Option-B	Detach audio from a clip
Command-Z	Undo the previous command

Keyboard Shortcut	Action
Command-Shift-Z	Redo, revoking the undo command
Command-M	Minimize the frontmost window to the Dock
1	Go to Library view (the default main window view)
2	Go to Projects view
Command-Shift-1	Show or hide the Libraries list
Command-1	Show my media in the browser
Command-2	Show audio in the browser
Command-3	Show titles in the browser
Command-4	Show maps and backgrounds in the browser
Command-5	Show sound effects in the browser
Command-6	Show transitions in the browser
Command-Shift-F	Play the selected item full screen

Image Capture

Version 8.0

Keyboard Shortcut	Action
Command-H	Hide this app
Command-Option-H	Hide all other apps
Command-Q	Quit this app
Command-W	Close the frontmost window
Command-Z	Undo the previous command
Command-Shift-Z	Redo, revoking the undo command
Command-X	Cut the selected text or item and copy it to the clipboard
Command-C	Copy the selected text or item to the clipboard
Command-V	Paste the contents of the clipboard
Command-A	Select all items
Press Function Twice	Start voice dictation
Command-Control-Space Bar	Show the Character Viewer, which you can choose emoji and other symbols
Command-M	Minimize the frontmost window to the Dock
Control-Shift-Tab	Show previous tab
Control-Tab	Show next tab
Command-Shift-Backslash	Show all tabs
Command-Option-L	Scan results

Keynote

Version 10.0

General Keyboard Shortcuts

Keyboard Shortcut	Action
Press Function Twice	Start voice dictation
Command-N	Open the theme chooser
Command-Option-N	Open the theme chooser and show the Language pop-up menu
Escape	Close the theme chooser
Command-O	Open an existing presentation
Command-S	Save a presentation
Command-Option-Shift-S	Save the current document by specifying the name and location
Command-Shift-S	Duplicate a presentation
Command-P	Print a presentation
Command-Shift-Question Mark	Open the Keynote User Guide
Command-W	Close the frontmost window
Command-Option-W	Close all windows
Command-M	Minimize the frontmost window to the Dock
Command-Option-M	Minimize all windows of this app to the Dock
Command-Control-F	Enter full-screen view
Command-Right Angle Bracket	Zoom in
Command-Left Angle Bracket	Zoom out
Command-Comma	Open the preferences window
Command-Shift-0	Zoom to selection
Command-Option-Shift-0	Zoom to fit content (including objects on the extended canvas) in the window

Keyboard Shortcut	Action
Command-Option-0	Fit slide in the window
Command-0	Return to actual size
Command-Shift-T	Show or hide the tab bar
Command-R	Show the presentation rulers
Command-Shift-V	Choose a file to insert
Command-Shift-C	Show the Colors window
Command-Option-T	Hide or show the toolbar
Command-Drag	Rearrange an item in the toolbar
Command-Drag away from the toolbar	Remove an item from the toolbar
Command-Option-I	Hide or show inspector sidebars
Command-Shift-L	Hide or show the object list
Command-A	Select all object types in the object list filter menu
Command-Shift-A	Deselect all object types in the object list filter menu
Control-Grave (`)	Open the next tab in the sidebar
Shift-Control-Grave (`)	Open the previous tab in the sidebar
Command-Shift-E	Enter or exit Edit Master Slides view
Command-Shift-N	Add a new master slide (from Edit Master Slides view)
Command-H	Hide this app
Command-Option-H	Hide other windows
Command-Z	Undo the previous command
Command-Shift-Z	Redo, revoking the undo command
Command-Q	Quit this app

Move Around in a Presentation

Keyboard Shortcut	Action
Command-Option-Q	Quit Keynote and keep windows open
Left Arrow	Move one character to the left
Right Arrow	Move one character to the right
Control-B	Move one character backward (works for left-to-right and right-to-left text)
Control-F	Move one character forward (works for left-to-right and right-to-left text)

Keyboard Shortcut	Action
Up Arrow	Move to the line above
Down Arrow	Move to the line below
Option-Left Arrow Option-Control-B	Move to the beginning of the current or previous word
Option-Right Arrow Option-Control-F	Move to the end of the current or next word
Command-Up Arrow	Move to the beginning of the current text area
Command-Down Arrow	Move to the bottom of the current text area
Command-Left Arrow	Move to the beginning of the current line
Command-Right Arrow	Move to the end of the current line
Option-Up Arrow	Move to the beginning of the current paragraph
Option-Down Arrow	Move to the end of the current paragraph
Command-E	Find the selected item in the presentation
Command-J	Jump to a selection in a presentation
Function-Up Arrow Home	Scroll to the beginning of the slide
Function-Down Arrow End	Scroll to the end of the slide
Control-L	Center the insertion point in the app window
Function-Down Arrow Page Down	Move to the next slide
Function-Up Arrow Page Up	Move to the previous slide
Function-Left Arrow Home	Move to the first slide
Function-Right Arrow End	Move to the last slide
Command-Control-G	Go to a specific slide

Text Selection

Keyboard Shortcut	Action
Command-A	Select all objects and text
Command-Shift-A	Deselect all objects and text

Keyboard Shortcut	Action
Click in the text, then Shift-Click in another location in the text	Extend the text selection
Shift-Right Arrow	Extend the selection one character to the right
Shift-Left Arrow	Extend the selection one character to the left
Option-Shift-Right Arrow	Extend the selection to the end of the current word, then to the end of subsequent words
Option-Shift-Left Arrow	Extend the selection to the beginning of the current word
Command-Shift-Right Arrow	Extend the selection to the end of the current line
Command-Shift-Left Arrow	Extend the selection to the beginning of the current line
Shift-Up Arrow	Extend the selection to the line above
Shift-Down Arrow	Extend the selection to the line below
Option-Shift-Up Arrow	Extend the selection to the beginning of the current paragraph
Option-Shift-Down Arrow	Extend the selection to the end of the current paragraph
Command-Shift-Up Arrow Shift-Home	Extend the selection to the beginning of the text
Command-Shift-Down Arrow Shift-End	Extend the selection to the end of the text

Format Text

Keyboard Shortcut	Action
Command-T	Show the Fonts window
Command-Shift-C	Show the Colors window
Command-B	Apply boldface to selected text
Command-I	Apply italic to selected text
Command-U	Apply underline to selected text
Delete	Delete the previous character or selection
Function-Delete Forward Delete	Delete the next character or selection
Option-Delete	Delete the word before the insertion point
Option-Forward Delete	Delete the word after the insertion point
Control-K	Delete the text between the insertion point and the next paragraph break
Command-Plus Sign	Make the font size bigger

Keyboard Shortcut	Action
Command-Minus Sign	Make the font size smaller
Command-Option-Left Bracket	Decrease the space between selected characters
Command-Option-Right Bracket	Increase the space between selected characters
Command-Control-Shift-Plus Sign	Make the text superscript
Command-Control-Minus Sign	Make the text subscript
Command-Shift-Left Curly Bracket	Align the text flush left
Command-Shift-Right Curly Bracket	Align the text flush right
Command-Shift-Vertical Bar	Center the text
Command-Option-Shift-Vertical Bar	Align the text flush left and flush right (justify)
Command-Left Bracket	Decrease the indent level of a block of text or a list item
Command-Right Bracket	Increase the indent level of a block of text or a list item
Shift-Tab	Decrease the indent level of a list item or headline
Tab	Increase the indent level of a list item or headline
Command-K	Turn text into a link
Command-X	Cut the selection
Command-C	Copy the selection
Command-Option--C	Copy the paragraph style
Command-V	Paste the selection
Command-Option-V	Paste the paragraph style
Command-Option-Shift-V	Paste and match the style of the destination text
Shift-Drag or Command-Drag	Add a range to (or remove it from) the selection
Option-Space Bar	Insert a non-breaking space
Shift-Return	Insert a line break (soft return)
Return	Insert a paragraph break
Control-O	Insert a new line after the insertion point
Command-Control-Space Bar	Show the Character Viewer, which you can choose emoji and other symbols
Control-T	Transpose the characters on either side of the insertion point
Assign a shortcut key	Apply a paragraph, character, or list style using your own shortcut
Command-Option-E	Insert an equation

Find and Delete Text, Comments, and Check Spelling

Keyboard Shortcut	Action
Command-F	Find items in a document or app
Command-G	Find again: find the next occurrence of the item already found (while in the Find window)
Command-Shift-G	Find the previous occurrence (while in the Find window)
Command-E	Place the selected text in the Find & Replace text field
Return	Replace text
Command-J	Scroll the window to show the selected text or object
Escape	Hide the Find window
Command-Control-D	Look up the word at the insertion point
Option-Escape	Display a list of words to complete the selected word
Command-Semicolon	Check spelling and grammar
Command-Shift-Colon	Show the "Spelling and grammar" window
Command-Shift-K	Open a new comment for the selected text, object, or table cell
Command-Return	Save a comment
Command-Option-K	Show the next comment
Command-Option-Shift-K	Show the previous comment

Manipulate Objects

Keyboard Shortcut	Action
Command-Shift-L	Show or hide the object list
Select one object, then press Command-A	Select all objects
Select one object, then press Command-Shift-A	Deselect all objects
Drag from a blank part of the slide around objects. Option-Drag to select objects outward from the starting point	Select objects by dragging
For Magic Mouse or a trackpad: Command-Option while scrolling	Zoom by scrolling
Command-Drag	Add or remove objects from the selection
Tab	Select the next object on the slide

Keyboard Shortcut	Action
Shift-Tab	Select the previous object on the slide
Command-Click Shift-Click	Select or deselect additional objects
Press an Arrow Key	Move the selected object one point
Press Shift and an Arrow Key	Move the selected object ten points
Press an Arrow Key	Move the selected object one screen pixel
Press Shift and an Arrow Key	Move the selected object ten screen pixels
Command-Option-C	Copy the graphic style of text
Command-Option-V	Paste the graphic style of text
Command-Shift-B	Send the selected object to the back
Command-Option-Shift-B	Send the selected object one layer back
Command-Shift-F	Bring the selected object to the front
Command-Option-Shift-F	Bring the selected object one layer forward
Command-Option-G	Group selected objects
Command-Option-Shift-G	Ungroup selected objects
Command-L	Lock selected objects
Command-Option-L	Unlock selected objects
Command-D or Option-Drag	Duplicate the object
Shift-Drag	Constrain the movement of the object to 45°
Command-Drag	Disable alignment guides while resizing
Option-Drag a selection handle	Resize the object from the center
Shift-Drag a selection handle	Constrain the aspect ratio when resizing the object
Option-Shift-Drag a selection handle	Constrain the aspect ratio when resizing the object from the center
Command-Drag a selection handle	Rotate the object
Press Shift while rotating	Rotate the object 45°
Command-Option-Drag a selection handle	Rotate the object around the opposite handle (instead of the center)
Command-Option-Shift-Drag a selection handle	Rotate the object 45° around the opposite handle (instead of the center)
Command-Drag	Turn off alignment guides while moving an object
Command-Shift-M	Mask or unmask the object
Return Enter	Hide mask controls

Keyboard Shortcut	Action
Control-Click the item	Open the shortcut menu for the selected item
Command-Return	Exit text editing and select the object
Command-Option-Control-I	Define the object as a media placeholder
Command-Option-Control-T	Define the selected text as a text placeholder

Modify Editable Shapes

Keyboard Shortcut	Action
Command-Option-Shift-P	Draw a custom shape with the Pen tool
Click the point, then press Delete	Delete a point of an editable shape
Command-Drag the midpoint of a line	Add a sharp point to an editable shape
Option-Drag the midpoint of a line	Add a Bézier point to an editable shape

Work with Tables

Keyboard Shortcut	Action
Option-Up Arrow	Add a row above the selected cells
Option-Down Arrow	Add a row below the selected cells
Option-Right Arrow	Add a column to the right of the selected cells
Option-Left Arrow	Add a column to the left of the selected cells
Select a cell in the bottom row, then press Option-Return	Insert a row at the bottom of the table
Select a cell in the right most column, then press Tab	Insert a column on the right of the table
Command-Option-Return	Select all rows that intersect the current selection
Command-Control-Return	Select all columns that intersect the current selection
Shift-Up Arrow Shift-Down Arrow	Select additional rows
Shift-Right Arrow Shift-Left Arrow	Select additional columns
Shift-Click	Select additional cells
Select a cell in the rightmost column, then press Tab	Move the cell selection to the beginning of the next row

Keyboard Shortcut	Action
Press Escape while dragging	Stop the reordering of rows or columns
Command-A	Select all content in a table
Delete	Delete the selected table, or the contents of selected cells
Shift-Drag the table	Constrain the movement of the table and snap to guides
Option-Drag the selected cell to another cell	Copy the contents of the selected cell into the destination cell
Command-Option-C	Copy cell style
Command-Option-V	Paste cell style
Command-Option-Shift-V	Paste and preserve the style of the destination cell
Select a cell, then press Return	Edit a cell
Press Option as you hover over a cell	Highlight the row and column for a cell
Space Bar	Open a pop-up menu in a selected cell
Command-Click a selected or unselected cell	Add a cell to (or remove it from) the selection
Command-Option-U	Auto-align cell content
Command-Return	Stop editing the cell and select the cell
Command-Return Twice	Stop editing the cell and select the table
Press an Arrow Key	Move the selected table one point
Press Shift and an Arrow Key	Move the selected table ten points
Select the table, then Shift-Drag a resize handle	Resize all columns in a table proportionately
Tab	Select the next cell or, if the last cell is selected, add a new row
Shift-Tab	Select the previous cell
Return	Select the cell below
Shift-Return	Select the cell above
Press an Arrow Key (from a selected cell)	Select the cell to the left, right, up, or down
Press Shift and an Arrow Key (from a selected cell)	Extend the cell selection by one cell
Command-Return	Select the parent of the current selection
Option-Tab	Insert a tab when editing text or a formula
Control-Return	Insert a line break (soft return) when editing text in a cell
Return	Insert a paragraph break (hard return) when editing text in a cell
Equal Sign	Open the formula editor for the selected non-formula cell

Keyboard Shortcut	Action
Option-Return	Open the formula editor for the cell containing a formula or formatted number
Command-Shift-V	Paste formula results
Return or Tab	In the formula editor, save changes
Escape	In the formula editor, discard changes
Command-Option-Left Arrow	Select the first populated cell in the current row
Command-Option-Right Arrow	Select the last populated cell in the current row
Command-Option-Up Arrow	Select the first populated cell in the current column
Command-Option-Down Arrow	Select the last populated cell in the current column
Command-Control-Shift-T	Insert the current time
Command-Control-Shift-D	Insert the current date
Command-Option-Delete	Delete selected rows
Command-Control-Delete	Delete selected columns
Shift-Tab	Select the table name
Command-Shift-V	Paste a formula result
Return	Select the first cell in a selected table
Command-Option-Shift-Left Arrow	Expand the current selection to include the first populated cell in the current row
Command-Option-Shift-Right Arrow	Expand the current selection to include the last populated cell in the current row
Command-Option-Shift-Up Arrow	Expand the current selection to include the first populated cell in the current column
Command-Option-Shift-Down Arrow	Expand the current selection to include the last populated cell in the current column
Command-Control-M	Merge selected cells
Command-Control-Shift-M	Unmerge selected cells
Command-Option-Control-Up Arrow	Add or remove the top border
Command-Option-Control-Down Arrow	Add or remove the bottom border
Command-Option-Control-Right Arrow	Add or remove the right border
Command-Option-Control-Left Arrow	Add or remove the left border
Command-Backslash	Turn on autofill mode
Command-Control-Backslash	Autofill from the column before
Command-Option-Backslash	Autofill from the row above

Edit Chart Data

Keyboard Shortcut	Action
Command-Shift-D	Show or hide the Chart Data Editor
Return	Complete a cell entry and move the selection down
Shift-Return	Complete a cell entry and move the selection up
Tab	Complete a cell entry and move the selection to the right
Shift-Tab	Complete a cell entry and move the selection to the left
Press the Left Arrow Right Arrow key	Move one character to the left or right
Press the Up Arrow Down Arrow key	Move to the beginning of text or to the end of text
Select the legend, then press an Arrow Key	Move the chart legend one point
Select the legend, then hold down Shift and press an Arrow Key	Move the chart legend ten points

Create Cell References in Formulas

Keyboard Shortcut	Action
Press Option and an Arrow Key	Navigate to and select a single cell
Press Option-Shift and an Arrow Key	Extend or shrink a selected cell reference
Press Command-Option and an Arrow Key	Navigate to the first or last non-header cell in a row or column
Option-Return	Insert a line break
Option-Tab	Insert a tab
Command-K Command-Shift-K	Move forward or backward through absolute and relative attributes of selected cell references
Command-Option-K Command-Option-Shift-K	Move forward or backward through absolute and relative attributes of the first and last cells of selected cell references

Use the Navigator View

Keyboard Shortcut	Action
Return Command-Shift-N	Create a new slide at same level as last selected slide
Tab	Indent selected slides to the right
Shift-Tab	Move indented slides to the left
Shift-Drag	Select multiple slides
Shift-Click	Extend or decrease the slide selection
Command-Click	Add (or remove) a single discontiguous slide from the selection
Option-Click the Add Slide button in the toolbar	Use the default master to create a new slide after the selected slide
Command-D	Duplicate a slide
Delete	Delete selected slides
Down Arrow	Move to the next slide
Up Arrow	Move to the previous slide
Right Arrow	Expand a slide group
Left Arrow	Collapse a slide group
Command-Shift-H	Skip a slide so it doesn't show in a presentation, or show a slide that's being skipped

Use the Light Table View

Keyboard Shortcut	Action
Right arrow	Move to the next slide
Left Arrow	Move to the previous slide
Shift-Right arrow	Extend the selection to the next slide
Shift-Left Arrow	Extend the selection to the previous slide
Command-Shift-Up Arrow	Extend the selection to the first slide
Command-Shift-Down Arrow	Extend the selection to the last slide
Command-Up Arrow	Select the first slide
Command-Down Arrow	Select the last slide

Play a Presentation and Use the Presenter Mode

Keyboard Shortcut	Action
Command-Option-P	Play a presentation
Option-Click the Play button in the toolbar	Play a presentation beginning with the first slide
Right Arrow Down Arrow	Advance to the next slide or build
Left Arrow Up Arrow	Go to previous slide
Shift-Right Arrow	Advance to the next build or slide without animation
Shift-Down Arrow Shift-Page Down	Advance to the next slide without builds and animations
Command-Shift-P	Show or hide presenter notes
Shift-Left Arrow Shift-Page Up	Go back to previous build
Z	Go back through previously viewed slides
F	Pause the presentation
B	Pause the presentation and show a black screen
W	Pause the presentation and show a white screen
C	Show or hide the pointer
S	Display the slide number
Press a slide number	Open the slide switcher
Plus Sign	Go to the next slide in the slide switcher
Minus Sign	Go to the previous slide in the slide switcher
Return	Go to the current slide and close the slide switcher
Escape	Close the slide switcher
X	Switch the primary and presenter displays
R	Reset timer
U	Scroll the presenter notes up
D	Scroll the presenter notes down
Command-Plus Sign	Increase note font size
Command-Minus Sign	Decrease note font size
Escape or Q	Quit presentation mode
H	Hide the presentation and switch to last app used

Keyboard Shortcut	Action
Question Mark or Forward Slash	Show or hide keyboard shortcuts
Home or Function-Up Arrow	Go to first slide
End or Function-Down Arrow	Go to last slide

Control a Video During a Presentation

Keyboard Shortcut	Action
Space Bar	Play the video
K	Pause or resume playing the video
J	Rewind the video (by frame, if it's paused)
L	Fast forward the video (by frame, if it's paused)
I	Jump to the beginning of the video
O	Jump to the end of the video

Mail

Version 13.4

Keyboard Shortcut	Action
Command-N	Start a new email
Command-Option-N	Open a new Mail viewer window
Command-Shift-A	Attach files to your email
Command-Shift-V	Paste text into your email as a quotation
Command-Option-I	Append selected emails to your email
Command-Option-B	Show the BCC address field in your email
Command-Option-R	Show the Reply-To address field in your email
Command-Shift-N	Get new emails
Command-Option-J	Erase junk mail
Command-Shift-D	Send emails
Command-R	Reply to the selected email
Command-Shift-R	Reply All to the selected email
Command-Shift-F	Forward the selected email
Command-Shift-E	Redirect the selected email
Command-Shift-U	Mark the selected emails as read
Command-Shift-J	Move the selected emails to the Junk mailbox
Command-Control-A	Archive the selected emails
Command-Control-L	Apply active Mail rules
Command-Shift-T	Format the current email as Plain Text or Rich Format
Command-0	Show the Mail viewer window
Command-Control-0	Show the Mail Activity window

Maps

Version 2.1

Keyboard Shortcut	Action
Command-L	Show your current location
Arrow keys	Move up or down, left or right
Option-Left Arrow (counterclockwise) Option-Right Arrow (clockwise)	Rotate the map
Command-Up Arrow	Return to the north-facing orientation
Command-Plus Sign	Zoom in
Command-Minus Sign	Zoom out
Command-1 Command-2	Switch between map and satellite views
Command-0	Show 3D map
Command-Shift-D	Drop a pin
Command-D	Add directions or a location to your Favorites

Messages
Version 13.0

Keyboard Shortcut	Action
Command-Comma	Open the preferences window
Command-H	Hide this app
Command-Option-H	Hide all other apps
Command-Q	Quit this app
Command-N	Start a new message
Command-0	Open the Messages window
Command-W	Close the frontmost window
Command-P	Print the conversation
Command-F	Search all conversations for matching text
Command-Option-K	Clear the transcript (delete a conversation without closing it)
Command-Control-Space Bar	Show the Character Viewer, which you can choose emoji and other symbols
Command-M	Minimize the frontmost window to the Dock
Command-Option-M	Minimize all windows of this app to the Dock
Command-Control-F	Enter full-screen view
Command-Plus Sign	Make the text bigger
Command-Minus Sign	Make the text smaller
Option-Return	Insert a line break (in a message)
Command-C	Copy the selected text
Command-V	Paste the contents of the clipboard
Command-Shift-Colon	Open the Spelling and grammar window
Command-Semicolon	Check the text field for spelling and grammar issues
Control-Tab	Select the next conversation

Keyboard Shortcut	Action
Control-Shift-Tab	Select the previous conversation
Command-Option-E	Send an email to a selected person in the conversation
Command-Shift-E	Show video effects (while in a video call in Messages)
Select a message, then press Delete	Delete a single message
Command-Option-Shift-W	Close all conversations

Music

Version 1.0

General Keyboard Shortcuts

Keyboard Shortcut	Action
Command-Comma	Open the preferences window
Command-Q	Quit this app
Command-E	Eject a CD
Command-?	Open Music Help menu
Command-Option (while opening Music)	Open a different music library

Play Songs, Music Videos, and More

Keyboard Shortcut	Action
Space Bar	Start playing or pause the selected song
Return	Play the currently selected song from the beginning
Command-Option-Right Arrow Left Arrow	Move forward or backward within a song
Command-Period	Stop playing the selected song
Right Arrow	When a song is playing, play the next song in a list
Left Arrow	When a song is playing, play the previous song in a list
Command-L	Show the currently playing song in the list
Command-Option-U	Show the Playing Next list
Option-Right Arrow Left Arrow	Listen to the next or previous album in a list
Command-Up Arrow	Increase the volume

Keyboard Shortcut	Action
Command-Down Arrow	Decrease the volume
Command-Option-E	Open the equalizer
Command-Shift-Right Arrow Command-Shift-Left Arrow	Go to the next or last chapter (if available)
Command-U	Stream audio file at a specific URL to Music

Create and Manage Playlists

Keyboard Shortcut	Action
Command-N	Create a new playlist
Command-Shift-N	Create a playlist from a selection of songs
Command-Option-N	Create a new Smart Playlist
Option-Space Bar	Start Genius Shuffle
Command-R	Refresh a Genius Playlist (when the playlist is selected)
Command-Delete	Delete the selected playlist without confirming that you want to delete it
Option-Delete	Delete the selected playlist and all the songs it contains from your library
Option-Delete	Delete the selected song from your library and all playlists

Manage Your Library and Media Files

Keyboard Shortcut	Action
Command-O	Add a file (import) to your library
Command-Shift-R	Show where a song file is located
Command-F	Select the search field
Command-Z	Undo your last typing change while editing an item's information
Command-X	Cut the selected song's information or artwork
Command-C	Copy the selected song's information or artwork
Command-V	Paste the selected song's information or artwork
Command-A	Select all the songs in the list
Command-B	Show or hide the column browser
Command-Shift-A	Deselect all the songs in the list

Keyboard Shortcut	Action
Command-Click the checkbox next to a song in the list	Select or deselect all the songs in a list

Change What You See

Keyboard Shortcut	Action
Command-Option-M Command-Shift-M	Open the MiniPlayer
Command-Shift-F	Open the Full Screen Player
Command-Control-F	Enter or exit full-screen view
Option-Click the green button in the top-left corner of the Music window	Switch between custom and maximum window sizes
Control-Click a column heading	Change the song information columns
Command-Forward Slash	Show or hide the status bar
Command-I	Open the Info window for the selected song
Command-N Command-P	In the Info window, see the information for the next or previous song in the list
Command-Shift-Left Bracket Command-Shift-Right Bracket	Go to the previous or next pane in the Info window
Command-J	Open the View Options window for the selected source
Command-T	Turn the visualizer on or off
Command-R	Refresh Apple Music or iTunes Store
Command-0	Open the Music window
Command-W	Close the frontmost window
Command-M	Minimize the frontmost window to the Dock
Command-H	Hide the Music window
Command-Option-H	Hide all other apps

Create and Manage Playlists

Keyboard Shortcut	Action
Type a word or phrase in the search field and press Option-Return	Initiate a search in the iTunes Store (from anywhere in Music)
Command-Right Bracket	Go to the next page in the iTunes Store
Command-Left Bracket	Go to the previous page in the iTunes Store
Command-R	Reload the current page

News

| Version 5.4

Keyboard Shortcut	Action
Command-L	Suggest more stories like the one you're currently reading
Command-D	Suggest fewer stories like the one you're currently reading
Command-S	Save or unsave a story
Command-Shift-L	Follow or unfollow the current channel or topic
Command-Shift-D	Block or unblock the current channel or topic
Command-Option-C	Copy the link for the current story
Command-R	Refresh a feed to show the latest stories
Command-Option-S	Show or hide the sidebar
Command-T	Show the table of contents for a magazine
Command-Plus Sign	Zoom in
Command-Minus Sign	Zoom out
Command-Option-Plus Sign	Make the text bigger
Command-Option-Minus Sign	Make the text smaller
Command-0	Reset content to its actual size
Command-Left Bracket	Close the current story or issue and return to the most recent feed
Right Arrow	Move to the next story or page
Left Arrow	Move to the previous story or page
Command-Up Arrow	Move to the top of a feed or story
Command-Down Arrow	Move to the bottom of a feed or story

Notes

| Version 4.7

General Keyboard Shortcuts

Keyboard Shortcut	Action
Command-N	Create a new note
Command-Shift-N	Create a new folder
Command-0	Show the main Notes window
Command-1	Show notes in a list
Command-2	Show notes in gallery view
Command-Option-F	Search all notes
Tab	Move between the sidebar, notes list, and search field
Return	Begin typing in the note selected in the notes list or gallery view
Command-P	Print a note
Command-Shift-A	Attach a file
Command-K	Create a link
Command-Option-T	Insert a table
Command-Shift-T	Apply Title format
Command-Shift-H	Apply Heading format
Command-Shift-J	Apply Subheading format
Command-Shift-B	Apply Body format
Command-Shift-M	Apply Monospaced format
Command-Shift-L	Apply Checklist format
Command-Plus Sign	Increase font size
Command-Minus Sign	Decrease font size

Keyboard Shortcut	Action
Command-Right Bracket Tab	Increase list level
Command-Left Bracket Shift-Tab	Decrease list level
Control-Return	Add a line break (soft return) to a list item or checklist
Option-Tab	Insert a tab character in a list item
Command-Shift-U	Mark or unmark a checklist item
Command-Control-Up Arrow	Move a list or checklist item up in the list
Command-Control-Down Arrow	Move a list or checklist item down in the list
Command-Shift-Right Angle Bracket	Zoom in on note's contents
Command-Shift-Left Angle Bracket	Zoom out on note's contents
Command-Shift-0	Change size of note's contents to default

Navigate in Tables

Keyboard Shortcut	Action
Return	Move down one row or add a new row at the bottom of the table
Option-Return	Add a new paragraph in a cell
Command-Option-Up Arrow	Add a new row above the current row
Command-Option-Down Arrow	Add a new row below the current row
Command-Option-Right Arrow	Add a new column to the right of the current column
Command-Option-Left Arrow	Add a new column to the left of the current column
Tab	Move to the next cell to the right
Shift-Tab	Move to the next cell to the left
Option-Tab	Add a tab character in a cell
Shift-Left Arrow Shift-Right Arrow	Select a range of cells in a row
Shift-Up Arrow Shift-Down Arrow	Select a range of cells in a column
Command-A	Select the content of the current cell

Numbers

| Version 10.0

General Keyboard Shortcuts

Keyboard Shortcut	Action
Press Function Twice	Start voice dictation
Command-N	Open the template chooser
Command-Option-N	Open the template chooser and show the Language pop-up menu
Command-O	Open an existing spreadsheet
Escape	Close the template chooser
Command-S	Save a spreadsheet
Command-Option-Shift-S	Save the current document by specifying the name and location
Return	End editing the spreadsheet or sheet name
Command-Shift-S	Duplicate a spreadsheet
Escape	End editing the spreadsheet or sheet name and restore the original name
Command-P	Print a spreadsheet
Command-Shift-N	Add a new sheet
Command-Shift-Left Curly Bracket	Switch to the previous sheet
Command-Shift-Right Curly Bracket	Switch to the next sheet
Command-Option-Shift-Left Curly Bracket	Switch to the first sheet
Command-Option-Shift-Right Curly Bracket	Switch to the last sheet
Page Up	Scroll one page up in print preview
Page Down	Scroll one page down in print preview
Command-Option-P	Preview a sheet or spreadsheet
Command-Shift-Question Mark	Open the Numbers User Guide
Command-W	Close a window

Keyboard Shortcut	Action
Command-Option-W	Close all windows
Command-M	Minimize the frontmost window to the Dock
Command-Option-M	Minimize all windows of this app to the Dock
Command-Control-F	Enter full-screen view
Command-Right Angle Bracket	Zoom in
Command-Left Angle Bracket	Zoom out
Command-Comma	Open the preferences window
Command-Shift-0	Zoom to selection
Command-0	Return to actual size
Command-Shift-T	Show or hide the tab bar
Command-R	Show the spreadsheet rulers
Command-Shift-C	Show the Colors window
Command-Option-T	Hide or show the toolbar
Command-Drag	Rearrange an item in the toolbar
Command-Drag away from the toolbar	Remove an item from the toolbar
Command-Option-I	Hide or show the sidebar
Control-Grave Accent	Open the next tab of the sidebar
Shift-Control-Grave Accent	Open the previous tab of the sidebar
Command-H	Hide this app
Command-Option-H	Hide all other apps
Command-Z	Undo the previous command
Command-Shift-Z	Redo, revoking the undo command
Command-Q	Quit this app
Command-Option-Q	Quit Numbers and keep windows open
Command-1 through Command-7	Select one of the first seven sheets

Move Around in a Spreadsheet

Keyboard Shortcut	Action
Left Arrow	Move one character to the left
Right Arrow	Move one character to the right

Keyboard Shortcut	Action
Control-B	Move one character backward (works for left-to-right and right-to-left text)
Control-F	Move one character forward (works for left-to-right and right-to-left text)
Up Arrow	Move to the line above
Down Arrow	Move to the line below
Option-Left Arrow Option-Control-B	Move to the beginning of the current or previous word
Option-Right Arrow Option-Control-F	Move to the end of the current or next word
Command-Up Arrow	Move to the beginning of the current text area
Command-Down Arrow	Move to the bottom of the current text area
Command-Left Arrow	Move to the beginning of the current line
Command-Right Arrow	Move to the end of the current line
Option-Up Arrow	Move to the beginning of the current paragraph
Option-Down Arrow	Move to the end of the current paragraph
With the Find window open, select text, then press Command-E	Find the selected item in the spreadsheet
Command-J	Jump to a selection in a spreadsheet
Page Up	Scroll up the sheet
Page Down	Scroll down the sheet
Home Function-Up Arrow	Scroll to the beginning of the sheet
End Function-Down Arrow	Scroll to the end of the sheet
Control-L	Center the insertion point in the app window
Control-V	Move down a page

Select Text

Keyboard Shortcut	Action
Double-click the word	Select a word
Triple-click in the paragraph	Select a paragraph
Command-A	Select all objects and text
Command-Shift-A	Deselect all objects and text

Keyboard Shortcut	Action
Click in the text, then Shift-Click in another location in the text	Extend the text selection
Shift-Right Arrow	Extend the selection one character to the right
Shift-Left Arrow	Extend the selection one character to the left
Option-Shift-Right Arrow	Extend the selection to the end of the current word, then to the end of subsequent words
Option-Shift-Left Arrow	Extend the selection to the beginning of the current word
Command-Shift-Right Arrow	Extend the selection to the end of the current line
Command-Shift-Left Arrow	Extend the selection to the beginning of the current line
Shift-Up Arrow	Extend the selection to the line above
Shift-Down Arrow	Extend the selection to the line below
Option-Shift-Up Arrow	Extend the selection to the beginning of the current paragraph
Option-Shift-Down Arrow	Extend the selection to the end of the current paragraph
Command-Shift-Up Arrow Shift-Home	Extend the selection to the beginning of the text
Command-Shift-Down Arrow Shift-End	Extend the selection to the end of the text

Format Text

Keyboard Shortcut	Action
Command-T	Show the Fonts window
Command-Shift-C	Show the Colors window
Command-B	Apply boldface to selected text
Command-I	Apply italic to selected text
Command-U	Apply underline to selected text
Delete or Control-H	Delete the previous character or selection
Control-D Forward Delete	Delete the next character or selection
Option-Delete	Delete the word before the insertion point
Option-Forward Delete	Delete the word after the insertion point
Control-K	Delete the text between the insertion point and the next paragraph break
Command-Plus Sign	Make the font size bigger

Keyboard Shortcut	Action
Command-Minus Sign	Make the font size smaller
Command-Option-Left Bracket	Decrease the space between selected characters
Command-Option-Right Bracket	Increase the space between selected characters
Command-Control-Shift-Plus Sign	Make the text superscript
Command-Control-Minus Sign	Make the text subscript
Command-Left Bracket	Decrease the indent level of a block of text or a list item
Command-Right Bracket	Increase the indent level of a block of text or a list item
Shift-Tab	Decrease the indent level of a list item or headline
Tab	Increase the indent level of a list item or headline
Command-K	Turn text into a link
Command-X	Cut the selection
Command-C	Copy the selection
Command-Option-C	Copy the paragraph style
Command-V	Paste the selection
Command-Option-V	Paste the paragraph style
Command-Option-Shift-V	Paste and match the style of the destination text
Shift-Drag Command-Drag	Add a range to (or remove it from) the selection
Option-Space Bar	Insert a non-breaking space
Shift-Return	Insert a line break (soft return)
Return	Insert a paragraph break
Control-O	Insert a new line after the insertion point
Command-Control-Space Bar	Show the Character Viewer, which you can choose emoji and other symbols
Control-T	Transpose the characters on either side of the insertion point
Command-Option-E	Insert an equation
Command-Control-Shift-T	Insert the current time
Command-Control-Shift-D	Insert the current date

Find and Delete Text, Comments, and Check Spelling

Keyboard Shortcut	Action
Delete	Delete the previous character or selection
Function-Delete Forward Delete	Delete the next character or selection
Command-F	Find items in a document or app
Command-G	Find again: find the next occurrence of the item already found (while in the Find window)
Command-Shift-G	Find the previous occurrence (while in the Find window)
Command-E	Place the selected text in the Find & Replace text field
Return	Replace text
Command-J	Scroll the window to show the selected text or object
Escape	Hide the Find window
Command-Control-D	Look up the word at the insertion point
Option-Escape	Display a list of words to complete the selected word
Command-Semicolon	Check spelling and grammar
Command-Shift-Colon	Show the Spelling and grammar window
Command-Shift-K	Open a new comment for the selected text, object, or table cell
Command-Return	Save a comment
Command-Option-K	Show the next comment
Command-Option-Shift-K	Show the previous comment

Manipulate Objects

Keyboard Shortcut	Action
Select one object, then press Command-A	Select all objects
Select one object, then press Command-Shift-A	Deselect all objects
Drag from a blank part of the sheet around objects. Option-Drag to select objects outward from the starting point	Select objects by dragging
Command-Option-Scroll (available with a Magic Mouse or a trackpad only)	Scroll zoom

Keyboard Shortcut	Action
Command-Drag	Add or remove objects from the selection
Tab	Select the next object on the sheet
Shift-Tab	Select the previous object on the sheet
Command-Click Shift-Click	Select or deselect additional objects
Drag	Move selected objects
Arrow Keys	Move the selected object one point
Shift and Arrow Keys	Move the selected object ten points
Arrow Keys	Move the selected object one screen pixel
Shift and an Arrow Key	Move the selected object ten screen pixels
Command-Option-C	Copy the graphic style
Command-Option-V	Paste the graphic style
Press Option and click a shape or text box style in the sidebar	Apply the shape style, but not the text style
Command-Shift-B	Send the selected object to the back
Command-Option-Shift-B	Send the selected object one layer back
Command-Shift-F	Bring the selected object to the front
Command-Option-Shift-F	Bring the selected object one layer forward
Command-Option-G	Group selected objects
Command-Option-Shift-G	Ungroup selected objects
Double-click the object	Select an object in a group
Tab	Select the next object in a group
Shift-Tab	Select the previous object in a group
With an object in a group selected, press Command-Return	End editing an object and select the group
Command-L	Lock selected objects
Command-Option-L	Unlock selected objects
Command-D Option-Drag	Duplicate the object
Shift-Drag	Constrain the movement of the object to 45°
Command-Drag	Disable alignment guides while resizing
Option-Drag a selection handle	Resize the object from the center
Shift-Drag a selection handle	Constrain the aspect ratio when resizing the object

Keyboard Shortcut	Action
Option-Shift-Drag a selection handle	Constrain the aspect ratio when resizing the object from the center
Command-Drag a selection handle	Rotate the object
Press Shift while rotating	Rotate the object 45°
Command-Option-Drag a selection handle	Rotate the object around the opposite handle (instead of the center)
Command-Option-Shift-Drag a selection handle	Rotate the object 45° around the opposite handle (instead of the center)
Command-Drag	Turn off alignment guides while moving an object
Command-Shift-M	Mask or unmask the object
Return Enter	Hide mask controls
Control-Click the item	Open the shortcut menu for the selected item
Command-Return	Exit text editing and select the object

Modify Editable Shapes

Keyboard Shortcut	Action
Command-Option-Control-I	Define the object as a media placeholder
Command-Option-Shift-P	Draw a custom shape with the Pen tool
Click the point, then press Delete	Delete a point of an editable shape
Command-Drag the midpoint of a line	Add a sharp point to an editable shape
Option-Drag the midpoint of a line	Add a Bézier point to an editable shape

Work with Tables

Keyboard Shortcut	Action
Option-Up Arrow	Add a row above the selected cells
Option-Down Arrow	Add a row below the selected cells
Option-Right Arrow	Add a column to the right of the selected cells
Option-Left Arrow	Add a column to the left of the selected cells
Option-Drag in the bottom-right corner of the table	Add or remove rows and columns with content

Keyboard Shortcut	Action
Command-Option-Delete	Delete selected rows
Command-Control-Delete	Delete selected columns
Select a cell in the bottom row, then press Return	Insert a row at the bottom of the table
Select a cell in the right-most column, then press Tab	Insert a column on the right of the table
Command-Option-Return	Select all rows that intersect the current selection
Command-Control-Return	Select all columns that intersect the current selection
Shift-Up Arrow or Shift-Down Arrow	Select additional rows
Shift-Right Arrow or Shift-Left Arrow	Select additional columns
Shift-Click	Select additional cells
Escape while dragging	Stop the reordering of rows or columns
Command-Return	Select a table from a cell selection
Option-Return	Select the first cell in a selected table
Command-A	Select all content in a table
Delete	Delete the selected table, or the contents of selected cells
Shift-Drag the table	Constrain the movement of the table and snap to guides
Option-Drag the selected cell to another cell	Copy the contents of the selected cell into the destination cell
Command-Option-C	Copy cell style
Command-Option-V	Paste cell style
Command-Option-Shift-V	Paste and preserve the style of the destination cell
Option-Return	Edit a cell
Press Option as you hover over a cell	Highlight the row and column for a cell
Space Bar	Open a pop-up menu in a selected cell
Return Space Bar	Select a value in a pop-up menu in a selected cell
Space Bar Y N	Check or uncheck a checkbox in a selected cell
0 through 5	Set the number of stars for a selected star rating cell
Type a value that's within the slider range	Set the value for a slider in a selected cell
Command-Click a selected or unselected cell	Add a cell to (or remove it from) the selection

Keyboard Shortcut	Action
Command-Option-U	Auto-align cell content
Command-Return	Stop editing the cell and select the cell
Command-Return Twice	Stop editing the cell and select the table
Arrow Keys	Move the selected table one point
Shift and Arrow Keys	Move the selected table ten points
Select the table, then Shift-Drag a resize handle	Resize all columns in a table proportionately
Tab	Select the next cell or, if the last cell of a row is selected, add a new column
Shift-Tab	Select the previous cell
Return	Select the cell below
Shift-Return	Select the cell above
Press an Arrow Key (from a selected cell)	Select the cell to the left, right, up, or down
Press Shift and an Arrow Key (from a selected cell)	Extend the cell selection by one cell
Command-Return	Select the parent of the current selection
Option-Tab	Insert a tab when editing text or a formula
Control-Return	Insert a line break (soft return) when editing text in a cell
Return	Insert a paragraph break (hard return) when editing text in a cell
Control-Equal Sign	Open the formula editor with the contents of the selected cell
Control-Equal Sign	Convert the formula in the open formula editor to text
Equal Sign	Open the empty formula editor
Option-Return	Open the formula editor for the cell containing a formula or formatted number
Command-Shift-V	Paste formula results
Return Tab	In the formula editor, save changes
Escape	In the formula editor, discard changes
Command-Shift-F	Turn Filters on or off
Command-Shift-R	Apply sorting rules
Command-8	Collapse selected category groups
Command-9	Expand selected category groups
Command-Option-Left Arrow	Select the first populated cell in the current row
Command-Option-Right Arrow	Select the last populated cell in the current row

Keyboard Shortcut	Action
Command-Option-Up Arrow	Select the first populated cell in the current column
Command-Option-Down Arrow	Select the last populated cell in the current column
Shift-Tab	Select the table name
Command-Shift-V	Paste a formula result
Command-Option-Shift-Left Arrow	Expand the current selection to include the first populated cell in the current row
Command-Option-Shift-Right Arrow	Expand the current selection to include the last populated cell in the current row
Command-Option-Shift-Up Arrow	Expand the current selection to include the first populated cell in the current column
Command-Option-Shift-Down Arrow	Expand the current selection to include the last populated cell in the current column
Command-Control-M	Merge selected cells
Command-Control-Shift-M	Unmerge selected cells
Command-Option-Control-Up Arrow	Add or remove the top border
Command-Option-Control-Down Arrow	Add or remove the bottom border
Command-Option-Control-Right Arrow	Add or remove the right border
Command-Option-Control-Left Arrow	Add or remove the left border
Command-Backslash	Turn on autofill mode
Command-Control-Backslash	Autofill from the column before
Command-Option-Backslash	Autofill from the row above

Work with Charts

Keyboard Shortcut	Action
Command-Shift-D	Edit chart data references
Select legend, then press an Arrow Key	Move the chart legend one point
Select legend, then hold down Shift and press an Arrow Key	Move the chart legend ten points

Create Cell References in Formulas

Keyboard Shortcut	Action
Option and an Arrow Key	Navigate to and select a single cell
Option-Shift and an Arrow Key	Extend or shrink a selected cell reference
Command-Option and an Arrow Key	Navigate to the first or last non-header cell in a row or column
Option-Return	Insert a line break
Option-Tab	Insert a tab
Press Command-K Command-Shift-K	Specify absolute and relative attributes of selected cell references
Press Command-Option-K Command-Option-Shift-K	Specify absolute and relative attributes of the first and last cells of selected cell references

Pages

Version 10.0

General Keyboard Shortcuts

Keyboard Shortcut	Action
Press Function Twice	Start voice dictation
Command-N	Open the template chooser
Command-Option-N	Open the template chooser and show the Language pop-up menu
Escape	Close the template chooser
Command-O	Open an existing document
Command-S	Save a document
Command-Option-Shift-S	Save the current document by specifying the name and location
Command-Shift-S	Duplicate a document
Command-P	Print a document
Command-Shift-Question Mark	Open the Pages User Guide
Command-W	Close the frontmost window
Command-Option-W	Close all windows
Command-M	Minimize the frontmost window to the Dock
Command-Option-M	Minimize all windows of this app to the Dock
Command-Control-F	Enter full-screen view
Command-Right Angle Bracket	Zoom in
Command-Left Angle Bracket	Zoom out
Command-Shift-0	Zoom to selection
Command-0	Return to actual size
Command-Shift-T	Show or hide the tab bar
Command-R	Show or hide the ruler

Keyboard Shortcut	Action
Command-Shift-P	Open the Page Setup window
Command-Shift-L	Show or hide layout boundaries
Command-Shift-I	Show formatting characters (invisibles)
Command-Shift-V	Choose a file to insert
Command-Shift-C	Show the Colors window
Command-Option-T	Hide or show the toolbar
Command-Drag	Rearrange an item in the toolbar
Command-Drag away from the toolbar	Remove an item from the toolbar
Command-Option-I	Hide or show sidebars on the right side of the Pages window
Control-Grave Accent	Open the next tab in the sidebar
Shift-Control-Grave Accent	Open the previous tab in the sidebar
Command-H	Hide this app
Command-Option-H	Hide all other apps
Command-Z	Undo the previous command
Command-Shift-Z	Redo, revoking the undo command
Command-Comma	Open the preferences window
Command-Q	Quit this app
Command-Option-Q	Quit Pages and keep windows open

Move Around the Document

Keyboard Shortcut	Action
Left Arrow	Move one character to the left
Right Arrow	Move one character to the right
Control-B	Move one character backward (works for left-to-right and right-to-left text)
Control-F	Move one character forward (works for left-to-right and right-to-left text)
Up Arrow	Move to the line above
Down Arrow	Move to the line below
Option-Control-B	Move to the beginning of the current or previous word
Option-Left Arrow	Move to the left edge of the current word (works for left-to-right and right-to-left text)

Keyboard Shortcut	Action
Option-Control-F	Move to the end of the current or next word
Option-Right Arrow	Move to the right edge of the current word (works for left-to-right and right-to-left text)
Command-Up Arrow	Move the insertion point to the beginning of the current text area (document, text box, shape, or table cell)
Command-Down Arrow	Move the insertion point to the bottom of the current text area (document, text box, shape, or table cell)
Control-A Option-Up Arrow	Move to the beginning of the paragraph
Control-E Option-Down Arrow	Move to the end of the paragraph
Command-Left Arrow	Move to the left edge of the current line
Command-Right Arrow	Move to the right edge of the current line
Function-Up Arrow Page Up	Scroll up one page without moving the insertion point
Function-Down Arrow Page Down	Scroll down one page without moving the insertion point
Option-Page Up	Scroll up one page and move the insertion point
Control-V Option-Page Down	Scroll down one page and move the insertion point
Function-Left Arrow Home	Move to the beginning of the document without moving the insertion point
Function-Right Arrow End	Move to the end of the document without moving the insertion point
Control-L	Center the insertion point in the center of the app window
Command-Control-G	Go to a specific page

Select Text

Keyboard Shortcut	Action
Command-A	Select all objects and text
Command-Shift-A	Deselect all objects and text
Click in the text, then Shift-Click in another location in the text	Extend the text selection
Shift-Right Arrow	Extend the selection one character to the right

Keyboard Shortcut	Action
Shift-Left Arrow	Extend the selection one character to the left
Option-Shift-Right Arrow	Extend the selection to the end of the current word, then to the end of subsequent words
Option-Shift-Left Arrow	Extend the selection to the beginning of the current word
Command-Shift-Right Arrow	Extend the selection to the end of the current line
Command-Shift-Left Arrow	Extend the selection to the beginning of the current line
Shift-Up Arrow	Extend the selection to the line above
Shift-Down Arrow	Extend the selection to the line below
Option-Shift-Up Arrow	Extend the selection to the beginning of the current paragraph
Option-Shift-Down Arrow	Extend the selection to the end of the current paragraph
Command-Shift-Up Arrow Shift-Home	Extend the selection to the beginning of the text
Command-Shift-Down Arrow Shift-End	Extend the selection to the end of the text

Format Text

Keyboard Shortcut	Action
Command-T	Show the Fonts window
Command-Shift-C	Show the Colors window
Command-B	Apply boldface to selected text
Command-I	Apply italic to selected text
Command-U	Apply underline to selected text
Delete or Control-H	Delete the previous character or selection
Control-D or Forward Delete	Delete the next character or selection
Option-Delete	Delete the word before the insertion point
Option-Forward Delete	Delete the word after the insertion point
Control-K	Delete the text between the insertion point and the next paragraph break
Command-Plus Sign	Make the font size bigger
Command-Minus Sign	Make the font size smaller
Command-Option-Left Bracket	Decrease (tighten) the space between selected characters
Command-Option-Right Bracket	Increase (loosen) the space between selected characters
Command-Control-Shift-Plus Sign	Make the text superscript

Keyboard Shortcut	Action
Command-Control-Minus Sign	Make the text subscript
Command-Option-E	Insert an equation
Command-Control-Shift-T	Insert the current time
Command-Control-Shift-D	Insert the current date
Command-Left Curly Bracket	Align the text flush left
Command-Vertical Bar	Center the text
Command-Right Curly Bracket	Align the text flush right
Command-Option-Vertical Bar	Align the text flush left and flush right (justify)
Command-Left Bracket	Decrease the indent level of a block of text or a list item
Command-Right Bracket	Increase the indent level of a block of text or a list item
Shift-Tab	Decrease the indent level of a list item
Tab	Increase the indent level of a list item
Command-K	Turn text into a link
Command-Option-B	Add a bookmark
Command-X	Cut the selection
Command-C	Copy the selection
Command-Option-C	Copy the paragraph style
Command-V	Paste the selection
Command-Option-V	Paste the paragraph style
Command-Option-Shift-V	Paste and match the style of the destination text
Command-Option-C	Copy the graphic style of text
Command-Option-V	Paste the graphic style of text
Shift-Drag	Add a range to (or remove it from) the selection
Option-Space Bar	Insert a non-breaking space
Shift-Return	Insert a line break (soft return)
Return	Insert a paragraph break
Control-O	Insert a new line after the insertion point
Function-Command-Return	Insert a page break
Command-Control-Space Bar	Show the Character Viewer, which you can choose emoji and other symbols
Control-T	Transpose the characters on either side of the insertion point
Shift-Command-Option-E	Add an End Note bibliography

Find and Delete Text, Comments, and Check Spelling

Keyboard Shortcut	Action
Delete	Delete the previous character or selection
Function-Delete Forward Delete	Delete the next character or selection
Command-F	Find items in a document or app
Command-G	Find again: find the next occurrence of the item already found (while in the Find window)
Command-Shift-G	Find the previous occurrence (while in the Find window)
Command-E	Place the selected text in the Find & Replace text field
Return	Replace text
Command-J	Scroll the window to show the selected text or object
Escape	Hide the Find window
Command-Control-D	Look up the word at the insertion point
Option-Escape	Display a list of words to complete the selected word
Command-Semicolon	Check spelling and grammar
Command-Shift-Colon	Show the "Spelling and grammar" window
Command-Shift-H	Highlight text
Command-Shift-K	Open a new comment for the selected text, object, or table cell
Command-Return	Save a comment
Command-Option-K	Show the next comment
Command-Option-Shift-K	Show the previous comment
Command-Option-A	Accept a change (when change tracking is on)
Command-Option-R	Reject a change (when change tracking is on)
Command-Shift-W	Show or hide word count
Command-Shift-E	Enter or exit edit master page view

Manipulate Objects

Keyboard Shortcut	Action
Command-A	Select all objects
Command-Shift-A	Deselect all objects

Keyboard Shortcut	Action
Command-Option-scroll (for Magic Mouse or a trackpad)	Scroll zoom
Command-Drag	Add or remove objects from the selection
Shift-Tab	Select the previous object on the page
Command-Click Shift-Click	Select or deselect additional objects
Drag	Move selected objects
Press an Arrow Key	Move the selected object one point
Press Shift and an Arrow Key	Move the selected object ten points
Press an Arrow Key	Move the selected object one screen pixel
Press Shift and an Arrow Key	Move the selected object ten screen pixels
Command-Option-C	Copy the graphic style
Command-Option-V	Paste the graphic style
Option-Click the shape style in the sidebar on the right side of the Pages window	Apply the shape style but not its text style
Command-Shift-B	Send the selected object to the back
Command-Option-Shift-B	Send the selected object one layer back
Command-Shift-F	Bring the selected object to the front
Command-Option-Shift-F	Bring the selected object one layer forward
Command-Option-G	Group selected objects
Command-Option-Shift-G	Ungroup selected objects
Tab	Select the next object in a group
Shift-Tab	Select the previous object in a group
Select an object in the group, then press Command-Return	End editing an object, then select the group
Command-L	Lock selected objects
Command-Option-L	Unlock selected objects
Option-Arrow Key Option-Drag	Duplicate the object
Shift-Drag	Constrain the movement of the object horizontally, vertically, or diagonally (45°)
Command-Drag	Disable alignment guides while moving or resizing an object
Option-Drag a selection handle	Resize the object from the center

Keyboard Shortcut	Action
Shift-Drag a selection handle	Constrain the aspect ratio when resizing the object
Option-Shift-Drag a selection handle	Constrain the aspect ratio when resizing the object from the center
Command-Drag a selection handle	Rotate the object
Press Shift while rotating	Rotate the object 45°
Command-Option-Drag a selection handle	Rotate the object around the opposite handle (instead of the center)
Command-Option-Shift-Drag a selection handle	Rotate the object 45° around the opposite handle (instead of the center)
Command-Shift-M	Mask or unmask the image
Return Enter	Hide image mask controls
Control-Click the item	Open the shortcut menu for the selected item
Command-Return	Exit text editing and select the object
Command-Shift-V	Choose an object to insert
Command-Option-Control-T	Define the selected text as a text placeholder
Command-Option-Control-I	Define the image or movie as a media placeholder

Modify Editable Shapes

Keyboard Shortcut	Action
Command-Option-Shift-P	Draw a custom shape with the Pen tool
Click the point, then press Delete	Delete a point of an editable shape
Command-Drag the midpoint of a line	Add a sharp point to an editable shape
Option-Drag the midpoint of a line	Add a Bézier point to an editable shape

Work with Tables

Keyboard Shortcut	Action
Option-Up Arrow	Add a row above the selected cells
Option-Down Arrow	Add a row below the selected cells
Option-Right Arrow	Add a column to the right of the selected cells
Option-Left Arrow	Add a column to the left of the selected cells

Keyboard Shortcut	Action
Option-Return	Insert a row at the bottom of the table
Command-Option-Return	Select all rows that intersect the current selection
Command-Control-Return	Select all columns that intersect the current selection
Shift-Up Arrow Shift-Down Arrow	Select additional rows
Shift-Right Arrow Shift-Left Arrow	Select additional columns
Shift-Click	Select additional cells
Select a cell in the rightmost column, then press Tab	Move the cell selection to the beginning of the next row
Escape while dragging	Stop the reordering of rows or columns
Command-Return	Select a table from a cell selection
Select a cell, then press Command-A	Select all content in a table
Delete	Delete the selected table, or the contents of selected cells
Press a cell, then Option-Drag it to another cell	Copy the contents of the selected cell into the destination cell
Command-Option-C	Copy cell style
Command-Option-V	Paste cell style
Command-Option-Shift-V	Paste and preserve the style of the destination cell
Shift-Click in the destination cell	Extend the selection from the selected cell to the destination cell
Command-Click a selected or unselected cell	Add a cell to (or remove it from) the selection
Return Enter	Begin text editing in a selected cell
Command-Option-U	Auto-align cell content
Command-Return	Stop editing the cell and select the cell
Command-Return Twice	Stop editing the cell and select the table
Press an Arrow Key	Move the selected table one point
Press Shift and an Arrow Key	Move the selected table ten points
Shift-Drag the table	Constrain the movement of the table horizontally, vertically, or diagonally
Select the table, then Shift-Drag a resize handle	Resize all columns in a table proportionately
Press an Arrow Key (from a selected cell)	Select the next cell to the left, right, up, or down
Press Shift and an Arrow Key	Extend the current cell selection by one cell

Keyboard Shortcut	Action
Tab	Select the next cell
Shift-Tab	Select the previous cell
Option-Tab	Insert a tab when editing text or a formula
Control-Return	Insert a line break (soft return) when editing text in a cell
Return	Insert a paragraph break (hard return) when editing text in a cell
Equal Sign	Open the formula editor for the selected non-formula cell
Return or Tab	In the formula editor, commit changes
Escape	In the formula editor, discard changes
Command-Option-Left Arrow	Select the first populated cell in the current row
Command-Option-Right Arrow	Select the first populated cell in the current row
Command-Option-Up Arrow	Select the first populated cell in the current column
Command-Option-Down Arrow	Select the last populated cell in the current column
Command-Option-Delete	Delete selected rows
Command-Control-Delete	Delete selected columns
Shift-Tab	Select the table name
Command-Shift-V	In a table, paste a formula result
Return	Select the first cell in a selected table
Command-Option-Shift-Left Arrow	Expand the selection to include the first populated cell in the current row
Command-Option-Shift-Right Arrow	Expand the selection to include the last populated cell in the current row
Command-Option-Shift-Up Arrow	Expand the selection to include the first populated cell in the current column
Command-Option-Shift-Down Arrow	Expand the current selection to include the last populated cell in the current column
Command-Control-M	Merge selected cells
Command-Control-Shift-M	Unmerge selected cells
Command-Option-Control-Up Arrow	Add or remove the top border
Command-Option-Control-Down Arrow	Add or remove the bottom border
Command-Option-Control-Right Arrow	Add or remove the right border
Command-Option-Control-Left Arrow	Add or remove the left border
Command-Backslash	Turn on autofill mode
Command-Control-Backslash	Autofill from the column before
Command-Option-Backslash	Autofill from the row above

Edit Chart Data

Keyboard Shortcut	Action
Command-Shift-D	Show or hide the Chart Data editor
Return	Complete a cell entry and move the selection down
Shift-Return	Complete a cell entry and move the selection up
Tab	Complete a cell entry and move the selection to the right
Shift-Tab	Complete a cell entry and move the selection to the left
Left Arrow Right Arrow	Move one character to the left or right
Up Arrow Down Arrow	Move to the beginning of text or to the end of text
Select the legend, then press an Arrow Key	Move the chart legend one point
Select the legend, then hold down Shift and press an Arrow Key	Move the chart legend ten points

Edit Tables

Keyboard Shortcut	Action
Press Option and an Arrow Key	Navigate to and select a single cell
Press Option-Shift and an Arrow Key	Extend or shrink a selected cell reference
Press Command-Option and an Arrow Key	Navigate to and select the first or last cell in a row or column
Select a reference and press Option-Return	Change a selected cell reference back to text
Press Command-K Command-Shift-K	Specify absolute and relative attributes of selected cell references
Press Command-Option-K Command-Option-Shift-K	Specify absolute and relative attributes of the first and last cells of selected cell references

Photo Booth

Version 11.0

Keyboard Shortcut	Action
Command-Return	Take a photo
Command-T	Trim a movie
Command-F	Flip a photo
Command-1	Show Photo view
Command-2	Show Effects view
Command-3	Show the last effect
Command-Right Arrow	Show the next page of Effects
Command-Left Arrow	Show the previous page of Effects
Command-Shift-R	Reset Effect

Photos

| Version 5.0

General Keyboard Shortcuts

Keyboard Shortcut	Action
Control-1	View photos
Control-2	View memories
Control-3	View favorites
Control-4	View people
Control-5	View places
Control-6	View recent additions to your library
Control-7	View imports
Command-1	View years (in Photos view)
Command-2	View months (in Photos view)
Command-3	View days (in Photos view)
Command-4	View all photos (in Photos view)
Command-1	View all memories (in Memories view)
Command-2	View favorite memories (in Memories view)
Space Bar	Open the selected photo
Space Bar Escape Key	Close an individual photo and see more photos
Arrow Keys	Scroll through photos in the Photos window
Left Arrow Right Arrow	See the next or previous photo in a day or album
Command-Up Arrow	Stop viewing a photo, project, album, or shared album
Option-S	Show or hide thumbnails below an open photo

Keyboard Shortcut	Action
Command-Comma	Open the preferences window
Command-P	Print the document
Command-W	Close the frontmost window and quit Photos
Command-M	Minimize the frontmost window to the Dock
Command-H	Hide this app
Command-Q	Quit this app

Edit Photos

Keyboard Shortcut	Action
Return	Open or close a selected photo in editing view
C Command-3	Crop a photo
A Command-1	Adjust a photo
F Command-2	Apply a filter
Command-Option-R (clockwise) Command-R (counterclockwise)	Rotate a photo
Command-E	Enhance a photo
Press and hold M	Show the original unadjusted photo while editing
Control-M	Show the unadjusted photo without additional editing changes, such as cropping or rotation
Right Arrow (press and hold to scroll through photos quickly)	Go to the next photo
Left Arrow (press and hold to scroll through photos quickly)	Go to the previous photo
Delete	Delete selected photos
Option-Space Bar	Play or pause a Live Photo or video
Command-F	Find photos
Z	Zoom between the current zoom level and 100 percent
Command-Plus Sign Command-Minus Sign	Zoom in or out
Command-L	Hide a selected photo

Keyboard Shortcut	Action
Command-Z	Undo the previous command
Command-Shift-Z	Redo, revoking the undo command
Control-Click	While in editing view or viewing thumbnails, open a shortcut menu to change or get information about a photo

Select and Deselect Photos

Keyboard Shortcut	Action
Command-A	Select all photos
Press and hold the Shift key and click the non-adjacent photo	Select all photos between the current selection and a nonadjacent photo
Select the first photo, then press and hold the Command key and click additional photos	Select photos that are not adjacent to one another
Press and hold the Command key and click the photos you want to deselect	Deselect specific photos in a group of selected photos
Command-Shift-A or click outside a photo	Deselect all photos

Organize Photos

Keyboard Shortcut	Action
Command-N	Create a new album
Command-Shift-K	Set a selected photo as the key photo for an album
Command-Option-N	Create a Smart Album
Command-Shift-N	Create a folder
Command-Plus Sign Command-Minus Sign	Change the size of photo thumbnails
Space Bar	Open or close a selected photo
Left Arrow Right Arrow	Move to the previous or next photo
Command-Control-F	Enter or leave full-screen view
Command-Shift-T	Show or hide titles
Command-L	Hide a selected photo
Command-I	Show or hide photo information in the Info window

Keyboard Shortcut	Action
Command-D	Duplicate a photo
Command-X	Cut the selected photo and copy it to the clipboard
Command-C	Copy a photo
Command-V	Paste a photo
Period	Make a photo a favorite
Command-K	Show or hide the Keyword Manager
Command-Delete	Delete a photo or item from the library
Delete	Remove a photo from an album (but not from the library)

Slideshows

Keyboard Shortcut	Action
Escape	Stop playing a slideshow
Space Bar	Pause or resume playing a slideshow
Right Arrow Left Arrow	Move through slides in a slideshow manually

Import and Export

Keyboard Shortcut	Action
Command-Shift-I	Import photos
Command-Shift-E	Export photos

Podcasts

Version 1.0

Keyboard Shortcut	Action
Command-Comma	Open the preferences window
Command-H	Hide this app
Command-Option-H	Hide all other apps
Command-Q	Quit this app
Command-N	Create a new station
Command-W	Close the frontmost window
Command-Shift-F	Enter or exit full-screen view
Command-M	Minimize the frontmost window to the Dock
Command-R	Refresh RSS feed updates
Command-F	Search your library or all podcasts
Up Arrow Down Arrow	When in a list of episodes, scroll up and down in the list
Shift-Up Arrow Shift-Down Arrow	When in a list of episodes, select episodes in the list (after you select an episode, Control-Click to do things like remove, save, and more)
Space Bar	Start playing or pause the selected episode
Command-Right Arrow Command-Left Arrow	Go to the next or previous episode in the Playing Next list
Command-Shift-Right Arrow Command-Shift-Left Arrow	Skip forward or backward within the selected episode
Command-Up Arrow	Increase the volume
Command-Down Arrow	Decrease the volume

Preview

Version 11.0

Keyboard Shortcut	Action
Down Arrow	Scroll down a line in a document, to the next item in the sidebar, or down through highlights and notes
Up Arrow	Scroll up a line in a document, to the previous item in the sidebar, or up through highlights and notes
Page Down	Scroll down one screen at a time or view the next image in the window
Page Up	Scroll up one screen at a time or view the previous image in the window
Option-Page Down	Move to next document in the window
Option-Page Up	Move to previous document in the window
Option-Down Arrow	Move to next page
Option-Up Arrow	Move to previous page
Command-Option-0	Zoom all images to actual size
Command-Option-9	Zoom all images to fit
Command-Option-Plus Sign	Zoom all images in
Command-Option-Minus Sign	Zoom all images out

QuickTime Player
Version 10.5

General Keyboard Shortcuts

Keyboard Shortcut	Action
Command-Option-N	New movie recording
Command-Option-Control-N	New audio recording
Command-Control-N	New screen recording
Command-O	Open a file
Command-L	Open location using a URL
Command-W	Close the frontmost window
Command-Shift-S	Duplicate the video
Command-M	Minimize the frontmost window to the Dock
Command-I	Show Movie Inspector
Command-Option-P	Show export progress

Movie Playback

Keyboard Shortcut	Action
Space Bar	Play or pause
Command-Return	Play or pause all movies
Left Arrow	Stop playback and go back one frame
Right Arrow	Stop playback and go forward one frame
Option-Left Arrow	Go to the beginning of a movie
Option-Right Arrow	Go to the end of a movie

Keyboard Shortcut	Action
Command-Left Arrow	Cycle through rewind speeds
Command-Right Arrow	Cycle through fast-forward speeds
Up Arrow	Turn the volume up
Down Arrow	Turn the volume down
Option-Up Arrow	Turn the volume up to the maximum level
Option-Down Arrow	Turn the volume down to the minimum level
Command-Option-L	Loop the movie

Change the View

Keyboard Shortcut	Action
Command-F	Enter full-screen view
Command-F or Escape	Exit full-screen view
Command-1	Display movie at actual size
Command-3	Fit the movie to the screen
Command-4	Fill the screen with the movie
Command-5	Display the movie in panoramic mode
Command-Plus Sign	Increase the movie size
Command-Minus Sign	Decrease the movie size

Movie Editing

Keyboard Shortcut	Action
Command-Z	Undo the previous command
Command-Shift-Z	Redo, revoking the undo command
Command-X	Cut the selected text or item and copy it to the clipboard
Command-C	Copy the selected text or item to the clipboard
Command-V	Paste the contents of the clipboard
Command-A	Select all items
Command-Shift-L	Rotate left
Command-Shift-R	Rotate right

Keyboard Shortcut	Action
Command-Shift-H	Flip video horizontally
Command-Shift-V	Flip video vertically
Command-Y	Split the clip
Command-T	Trim the clip at the selected point

Reminders

Version 7.0

Keyboard Shortcut	Action
Command-N	Create a new reminder
Command-Shift-N	Create a new list
Command-Right Bracket	Indent reminder
Command-Left Bracket	Outdent reminder
Command-E	Show all subtasks
Command-Shift-E	Hide all subtasks
Command-Shift-F	Flag reminder
Command-I	Show info
Command-Control-S	Hide or show sidebar
Command-Control-F	Enter or exit full screen
Command-W	Close the frontmost window and quit the app
Command-Q	Quit this app

Safari

Version 13.1

Keyboard Shortcut	Action
Press Option while you press an Arrow Key	Scroll in larger increments
Page Down Space Bar	Scroll down a screen
Page Up Shift-Space Bar	Scroll up a screen
Command-Up Arrow Home	Scroll to the top-left corner of the page
Command-Down Arrow End	Scroll to the bottom-left corner of the page
Tab	Highlight the next item on a webpage
Command-Shift-Backslash	Show all tabs
Command-Click a link	Open a page in a new tab
Command-Shift-Click a link	Open a page in a new tab, and make that tab the active tab
Control-Tab Command-Shift-Right Bracket	Make the next tab the active tab
Control-Shift-Tab ommand-Shift-Left Bracket	Make the previous tab the active tab
Command-1 through Command-9	Select one of your first nine tabs
Option-Click the Close button on the tab you want to leave open	Close all tabs except for one
Command-Shift-T	Reopen the last tab or window you closed
Press Option and hold down the Back or Forward button until the list appears	See a list of your recently visited pages by web address (URL)
Command-Home	Go to your homepage

Keyboard Shortcut	Action
Option-Click a link to the file	Download a linked file
Press Command-Plus Sign Command-Minus Sign	Zoom website content
Press Option while you choose View > Make Text Bigger or View > Make Text Smaller	Zoom website text
Command-Control-2	Show or Hide the Reading List sidebar
Command-Shift-D	Reading List: Add the current page
Shift-Click a link to the page	Reading List: Add a linked page
Control-Click the page summary in the sidebar, then choose Remove Item	Reading List: Remove a page
Command-Click the folder in the Favorites bar	Open all bookmarks from a folder in the Favorites bar
Drag the bookmark off the top of the bar	Remove a bookmark from the Favorites bar
Command-Control-1	Show or Hide the Bookmarks sidebar
Command-Click each bookmark and folder. Shift-Click to extend the selection	Select bookmarks and folders in the sidebar
Up Arrow Down Arrow	Select the next bookmark or folder
Space Bar	Open the selected bookmark
Space Bar Right Arrow	Open the selected folder
Space Bar Left Arrow	Close the selected folder
Select the bookmark, then press Return	Change the name or address of a bookmark
Return	Finish editing a bookmark name
Option-Click the New Folder button near the top-right corner	Create a folder containing the selected bookmarks and folders in bookmarks view
Control-Click the bookmark, then choose Delete	Delete a bookmark

Stickies

| Version 10.2

Keyboard Shortcut	Action
Command-H	Hide this app
Command-Option-H	Hide all other apps
Command-Q	Quit this app
Command-N	Create a new note
Command-W	Close the frontmost window
Command-P	Print the stick note
Command-X	Cut the selected text or item and copy it to the clipboard
Command-C	Copy the selected text or item to the clipboard
Command-V	Paste the contents of the clipboard
Command-Option-Shift-P	Paste and Match Style
Command-A	Select all items
Command-K	Add a link
Command-F	Find items in a document or app
Command-G	Find again: find the next occurrence of the item already found
Command-Shift-G	Find the previous occurrence
Command-E	Use selection for find
Command-J	Jump to selection
Command-Colon	Show Spelling and grammar
Command-Semicolon	Check document now for spelling
Press Function Twice	Start voice dictation

Keyboard Shortcut	Action
Command-Control-Space Bar	Show the Character Viewer, which you can choose emoji and other symbols
Command-T	Show the fonts pane
Command-B	Boldface the text
Command-U	Underline the text
Command-I	Italicize the text
Command-Plus Sign	Make text bigger
Command-Minus Sign	Make text smaller
Command-Shift-C	Show Colors
Command-Option-V	Paste the text style
Command-1	Yellow sticky note color
Command-2	Blue sticky note color
Command-3	Green sticky note color
Command-4	Pink sticky note color
Command-5	Purple sticky note color
Command-6	Gray sticky note color
Command-M	Collapse a sticky note
Command-Shift-M	Stick note window zoom
Command-Option-F	Make the sticky note float on top
Command-Option-T	Make the sticky note translucent
Command-Option-Z	Undo arrange
Command-Option-Shift-Z	Redo arrange

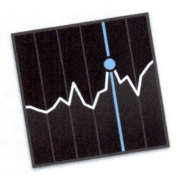

Stocks

Version 2.4

Keyboard Shortcut	Action
Command-Option-F	Search to add symbols
Delete	Remove symbol from watchlist
Command-S	Save story to News or unsave story
Command-Option-Plus Sign	Make text bigger
Command-Option-Minus Sign	Make text smaller
Command-0	Actual size
Command-Plus Sign	Zoom in to a story
Command-Minus Sign	Zoom out to a story
Command-Left Bracket	Go back
Right Arrow	Show the next story
Left Arrow	Show the previous story
Space Bar	Page up in story
Shift-Space Bar	Page down in story
Command-Up Arrow	Go to top of story, news feed, or watchlist
Command-Down Arrow	Go to bottom of story, news feed, or watchlist
Tab	Move focus from sidebar to news feed
Shift-Tab	Move focus from news feed to sidebar
Right Arrow	Show next story in news feed
Left Arrow	Show previous story in news feed

Keyboard Shortcut	Action
Enter Return	Open selected story
Down Arrow	Select next item in sidebar
Up Arrow	Select previous item in sidebar
Command-R	Refresh the page
Command-Q	Quit this app

TextEdit

Version 1.15

Keyboard Shortcut	Action
Command-Comma	Open the preferences window
Command-H	Hide this app
Command-Option-H	Hide all other apps
Command-Q	Quit this app
Command-N	Create a new TextEdit file
Command-O	Open a file
Command-W	Close the frontmost window
Command-S	Save the document
Command-Shift-S	Duplicate the document
Command-Option-P	Show properties
Command-Shift-P	Show page setup for printing
Command-P	Print the document
Command-Z	Undo the previous command
Command-Shift-Z	Redo, revoking the undo command
Command-X	Cut the selected text or item and copy it to the clipboard
Command-C	Copy the selected text or item to the clipboard
Command-V	Paste the contents of the clipboard
Command-Option-Shift-P	Paste and Match Style
Option-Escape	Complete the word
Command-A	Select all items

Keyboard Shortcut	Action
Command-Shift-A	Attach files
Command-K	Add a link
Command-F	Find items in a document or app
Command-G	Find again: find the next occurrence of the item already found
Command-Shift-G	Find the previous occurrence
Command-E	Use selection for find
Command-J	Jump to selection
Command-L	Select a line of text
Command-Colon	Show spelling and grammar
Command-Semicolon	Check the document for speeling now
Press Function Twice	Start voice dictation
Command-Control-Space Bar	Show the Character Viewer, which you can choose emoji and other symbols
Command-T	Show the fonts pane
Command-B	Boldface the text
Command-U	Underline the text
Command-I	Italicize the text
Command-Plus Sign	Make the text bigger
Command-Minus Sign	Make the text smaller
Command-Shift-C	Show Colors
Command-Option-V	Paste text style
Command-Left Curly Bracket	Align text to the left
Command-I	Center the text
Command-Right Curly Bracket	Align text to the right
Command-R	Show the ruler
Command-Control-R	Copy the ruler
Command-Control-V	Paste the ruler
Command-Shift-T	Make text plain text
Command-Shift-W	Wrap to the page

Keyboard Shortcut	Action
Command-0	Show actual size
Command-Shift-Period	Zoom in
Command-Shift-Comma	Zoom out
Command-Control-F	Enter full screen
Command-M	Minimize the frontmost window to the Dock
Control-Shift-Tab	Show the previous tab
Control-Tab	Show the next tab

TV

Version 1.0

Keyboard Shortcut	Action
Space Bar	Play or pause the selected episode
Command-Shift-Right Arrow Command-Shift-Left Arrow	Skip ahead (fast forward) or rewind the selected episode
Command-Up Arrow	Increase the volume
Command-Down Arrow	Decrease the volume
Command-Left Bracket	Go back
Command-Right Bracket	Go forward
Command-R	Reload the page
Command-N	Create a new playlist
Command-Shift-N	Create a playlist from a selection of songs
Command-Option-N	Create a new Smart Playlist
Option-Space Bar	Start Genius Shuffle
Command-R	Refresh a playlist (when the playlist is selected)
Command-O	Import a video file
Command-Delete	Delete the selected playlist without confirming that you want to delete it
Option-Delete	Delete the selected playlist and all the songs it contains from your library
Option-Delete	Delete the selected song from your library and all playlists
Command-Comma	Open the preferences window
Command-H	Hide this app
Command-Option-H	Hide all other apps

Keyboard Shortcut	Action
Command-Q	Quit this app
Command-Shift-L	View download activity
Command-0	Open the TV window
Command-W	Close the frontmost window
Command-M	Minimize the frontmost window to the Dock
Command-Option-F	Enter or exit full-screen view
Option-Click the green button in the upper-left corner of the TV window	Switch between custom and maximum window sizes
Command-Drag the resize control in the lower-right corner of the window	See the TV window resize while you're resizing it
Command-I	Open the Info window for the selected item
Command-N or Command-P	In the Info window, see the info for the next or previous item in the list
Command-J	Open the View Options window for the selected item
Command-Shift-F	Show filter field
Command-Forward Slash	Show or hide the status bar

Voice Memos

Version 2.1

Keyboard Shortcut	Action
Command-N	Record a voice memo
Space Bar	Play, pause, or resume a voice memo
Command-D	Duplicate a voice memo
Command-T	Trim a voice memo
Delete key	Delete a voice memo
Command-Z	Undo the previous command
Command-Shift-Z	Redo, revoking the undo command
Command-Comma	Open the preferences window
Command-M	Minimize the frontmost window to the Dock
Command-H	Hide this app
Command-Option-H	Hide all other apps
Command-Control-F	Enter full-screen view
Escape	Exit full-screen view
Command-Q Command-W	Quit this app

Classroom

Version 2.2

Keyboard Shortcut	Action
Command-Shift-N	Create a new class
Command-D	Invite students to class
Command-N	Create a new group
Command-Option-Delete	Remove a group
Command-T	Show the teacher info
Command-I	Show the class info
Command-Option-O	Start the class
Command-Delete	End the class
Command-O	Open the app
Command-G	Navigate a student
Command-Shift-H	Hide apps
Command-L	Lock a student's device
Command-B	Mute a student's device
Command-P	Start AirPlay
Command-Period	Assign iPads
Command-Forward Slash	Log Out of iPad
Command-Apostrophe	Reset Password
Command-1	View as Students
Command-2	View as Screens
Command-3	Show the inbox

Keyboard Shortcut	Action
Command-Arrow Down	View a student
Command-Arrow Up	Show all students
Command-Arrow Right	Show next student
Command-Arrow Left	Show previous student

Compressor

Version 4.4.6

Keyboard Shortcut	Action
Command-I	Add a file
Command-Option-I	Add a set of image sequence files
Command-Control-I	Add a set of surround sound files
Up Arrow	Navigate up the list of jobs (in the batch area)
Down Arrow	Navigate down the list of jobs (in the batch area)
Space Bar	Play or pause the video
J	Play the video in reverse
K	Stop playback
L	Play the video
I	Set the In point
O	Set the Out point
M	Add a marker
Option-C	Add a caption
Control-Semicolon	Go to the previous marker or In/Out point
Control-Apostrophe	Go to the next marker or In/Out point
Command-B	Start transcoding the batch
Command-1	Show the Current view
Command-2	Show the Active view
Command-3	Show the Completed view
Command-4	Show or hide the inspector pane

Keyboard Shortcut	Action
Command-5	Show or hide the Settings and Locations pane
Command-Shift-1	Show Settings
Command-Shift-2	Show Locations
Command-E	Show the Network Encoding Monitor
Command-Comma	Open the preferences window
Command-M	Minimize the frontmost window to the Dock
Command-W	Close the frontmost window
Command-Q	Quit this app

Final Cut Pro X
Version 10.4.8

General Keyboard Shortcuts

Keyboard Shortcut	Action
Command-H	Hide this app
Command-Option-H	Hide all other apps
Command-Option-K	Open the Command Editor
Command-M	Minimize the frontmost window to the Dock
Command-O	Open an existing library or a new library
Command-Comma	Open the preferences window
Command-Q	Quit this app
Command-Shift-Z	Redo, revoking the undo command
Command-Z	Undo the previous command
Delete	Delete the timeline selection, reject the browser selection, or remove a through edit
Command-F	Show or hide the Filter window (in the browser) or the timeline index (in the timeline)
Command-Option-3	Make the event viewer active
Command-I	Import media from a device, a camera, or an archive
Command-Control-J	Open the Library Properties inspector for the current library
Command-Delete	Move the selection to the Finder Trash
Command-N	Create a new project
Command-J	Open the Properties inspector for the current project
Control-Shift-R	Start all rendering tasks for the current project
Control-R	Start rendering tasks for the selection
Command-Shift-R	Reveal the selected event clip's source media file in the Finder

Editing

Keyboard Shortcut	Action
Option-Control-L	Adjust the audio volume across all selected clips to a specific dB value
Control-L	Adjust the audio volume across all selected clips by the same dB value
E	Add the selection to the end of the storyline
Control-Shift-Y	Add the selected clip to the audition
Option-Y	Create an audition with a timeline clip and a duplicate version of the clip, including applied effects
Command-Shift-Y	Duplicate the selected audition clip without applied effects
Shift-Y	Create an audition and replace the timeline clip with the current selection
Command-B	Cut the primary storyline clip (or the selection) at the skimmer or playhead location
Command-Shift-B	Cut all clips at the skimmer or playhead location
Command-Shift-G	Break the selected item into its component parts
Control-D	Change the duration of the selection
Control-Shift-T	Connect the default lower third to the primary storyline
Control-T	Connect the default title to the primary storyline
Q	Connect the selection to the primary storyline
Shift-Q	Connect the selection to the primary storyline, aligning the selection's end point with the skimmer or playhead
Command-C	Copy the selection
Command-Y	Create an audition from the selection
Command-G	Create a storyline from a selection of connected clips
Command-X	Cut the selection
1	Cut and switch the multicam clip to angle 1 of the current bank
2	Cut and switch the multicam clip to angle 2 of the current bank
3	Cut and switch the multicam clip to angle 3 of the current bank
4	Cut and switch the multicam clip to angle 4 of the current bank
5	Cut and switch the multicam clip to angle 5 of the current bank
6	Cut and switch the multicam clip to angle 6 of the current bank
7	Cut and switch the multicam clip to angle 7 of the current bank
8	Cut and switch the multicam clip to angle 8 of the current bank
9	Cut and switch the multicam clip to angle 9 of the current bank

Keyboard Shortcut	Action
Delete	Delete the timeline selection, reject the browser selection, or remove a through edit
Command-Option-Delete	Delete the selection and attach the connected clip or clips to the resulting gap clip
Command-Shift-A	Deselect all selected items
Command-D	Duplicate the browser selection
V	Enable or disable playback for the selection
Control-S	View audio and video separately for selected clips
Option-Control-S	Expand or collapse audio components for the selection in the timeline
Shift-X	Extend the selected edit point to the skimmer or playhead position
Shift-Down Arrow	In the browser list view, add the next item to the selection
Command-Control-Right-Arrow	In the timeline, add the next item to the selection
Shift-Up Arrow	In the browser list view, add the previous item to the selection
Option-Shift-Y	Dissolve the audition and replace it with the audition pick
W	Insert the selection at the skimmer or playhead position
Option-F	Insert a freeze frame at the playhead or skimmer location in the timeline, or connect a freeze frame from the skimmer or playhead location in the event to the playhead location in the timeline
Option-W	Insert a gap clip at the skimmer or playhead position
Command-Option-W	Insert the default generator at the skimmer or playhead position
Command-Option-Up Arrow	Lift the selection from the storyline and connect it to the resulting gap clips
Control-Hyphen	Lower the audio volume by 1 dB
Control-P	Move the playhead by entering a timecode value
Option-G	Create a new compound clip (if there's no selection, create an empty compound clip)
Option-Comma	Nudge the selected audio edit point left by one subframe, creating a split edit
Option-Shift-Comma	Nudge the selected audio edit point left by 10 subframes, creating a split edit
Option-Period	Nudge the selected audio edit point right by one subframe, creating a split edit
Option-Shift-Period	Nudge the selected audio edit point right by 10 subframes, creating a split edit
Option-Down Arrow	Nudge down the value of the selected keyframe in the animation editor
Comma	Nudge the selection one unit to the left

Keyboard Shortcut	Action
Shift-Comma	Nudge the selection 10 units to the left
Period	Nudge the selection one unit to the right
Shift-Period	Nudge the selection 10 units to the right
Option-Up Arrow	Nudge up the value of the selected keyframe in the animation editor
Y	Open the selected audition
Grave Accent	Temporarily override clip connections for the selection
D	Overwrite at the skimmer or playhead position
Shift-D	Overwrite from the skimmer or playhead position back
Command-Option-Down Arrow	Overwrite at the skimmer or playhead position in the primary storyline
Option-V	Paste the selection and connect it to the primary storyline
Command-V	Insert the clipboard contents at the skimmer or playhead position
Control-Shift-Left Arrow	Switch to the previous angle in the multicam clip
Option-Shift-Left Arrow	Switch to the previous audio angle in the multicam clip
Control-Left Arrow	Select the previous clip in the Audition window, making it the audition pick
Command-Shift-Left Arrow	Switch to the previous video angle in the multicam clip
Control-Equal Sign	Raise the audio volume by 1 dB
Shift-R	Replace the selected clip in the timeline with the browser selection
Option-R	Replace the selected clip in the timeline with the browser selection, starting from its start point
Shift-Delete	Replace the selected timeline clip with a gap clip
Command-A	Select all clips
C	Select the clip under the pointer in the timeline
Command-Up Arrow	Select the clip above the current timeline selection at the skimmer or playhead location
Command-Down Arrow	Select the clip below the current timeline selection at the skimmer or playhead location
Shift-Left Bracket	For audio/video clips in expanded view, select the left edge of the audio edit point
Left Bracket	Select the left edge of the edit point
Shift-Backslash	For audio/video clips in expanded view, select the left and right edges of the audio edit point
Backslash	Select the left and right edges of the edit point
Control-Backslash	For audio/video clips in expanded view, select the left and right edges of the video edit point

Keyboard Shortcut	Action
Control-Left Bracket	For audio/video clips in expanded view, select the left edge of the video edit point
Control-Shift-Right Arrow	Switch to the next angle in the multicam clip
Option-Shift-Right Arrow	Switch to the next audio angle in the multicam clip
Command-Right Arrow	Move the playhead and the selection to the next topmost timeline clip in the same role
Control-Right Arrow	Select the next clip in the Audition window, making it the audition pick
Command-Shift-Right Arrow	Switch to the next video angle in the multicam clip
Command-Left Arrow	Move the playhead and the selection to the previous topmost timeline clip in the same role
Shift-Right Bracket	For audio/video clips in expanded view, select the right edge of the audio edit point
Right Bracket	Select the right edge of the edit point
Control-Right Bracket	For audio/video clips in expanded view, select the right edge of the video edit point
Command-Shift-O	Set an additional range selection end point at the playhead or skimmer location
Command-Shift-I	Set an additional range selection start point at the playhead or skimmer location
Control-E	When an edit point is selected, show or hide the precision editor
N	Turn snapping on or off
Option-S	Solo the selected items in the timeline
Shift-1	Turn on audio/video mode to add the video and audio portion of your selection to the timeline
Shift-3	Turn on audio-only mode to add the audio portion of your selection to the timeline
Shift-2	Turn on video-only mode to add the video portion of your selection to the timeline
Command-Option-Control-C	Replace the selected captions with abutting single-line captions, one for each line of text in the original captions
Option-1	Switch the multicam clip to angle 1 of the current bank
Option-2	Switch the multicam clip to angle 2 of the current bank
Option-3	Switch the multicam clip to angle 3 of the current bank
Option-4	Switch the multicam clip to angle 4 of the current bank
Option-5	Switch the multicam clip to angle 5 of the current bank
Option-6	Switch the multicam clip to angle 6 of the current bank

Keyboard Shortcut	Action
Option-7	Switch the multicam clip to angle 7 of the current bank
Option-8	Switch the multicam clip to angle 8 of the current bank
Option-9	Switch the multicam clip to angle 9 of the current bank
G	Turn on or turn off the ability to build storylines when dragging clips in the timeline
Option-Right Bracket	Trim the end of the selected or topmost clip to the skimmer or playhead position
Option-Left Bracket	Trim the clip start point to the skimmer or playhead position
Option-Backslash	Trim clip start and end points to the range selection

Effects

Keyboard Shortcut	Action
Control-Shift-T	Connect a basic lower-third title to the primary storyline
Control-T	Connect a basic title to the primary storyline
Command-Option-E	Add the default audio effect to the selection
Command-T	Add the default transition to the selection
Option-E	Add the default video effect to the selection
Option-Delete	Reset the controls in the current Color Board pane
Command-Control-C	Switch to the Color pane in the Color Board
Command-Control-E	Switch to the Exposure pane in the Color Board
Command-Control-S	Switch to the Saturation pane in the Color Board
Command-Option-C	Copy the selected effects and their settings
Option-Shift-C	Copy the selected keyframes and their settings
Option-Shift-X	Cut the selected keyframes and their settings
Command-Option-B	Turn Balance Color corrections on or off
Command-Shift-M	Match the sound between clips
Command-Option-M	Match color between clips
Option-Tab	Navigate to the next text item
Command-Shift-V	Paste selected attributes and their settings to the selection
Command-Option-V	Paste effects and their settings to the selection
Option-Shift-V	Paste keyframes and their settings to the selection

Keyboard Shortcut	Action
Option-Shift-Tab	Navigate to the previous text item
Command-Shift-X	Remove selected attributes from the selection
Command-Option-X	Remove all effects from the selection
Command-R	Show or hide the retime editor
Shift-N	Set the selection to play at normal (100 percent) speed
Shift-H	Create a 2-second hold segment
Command-Option-R	Reset the selection to play forward at normal (100 percent) speed
Control-Shift-V	Show one effect at a time in the Video Animation editor

Marking

Keyboard Shortcut	Action
Option-C (or Option-Control-C if the caption editor is open)	Add a caption to the active language subrole at the playhead location
M	Add a marker at the location of the skimmer or playhead
Control-C	Change the browser filter settings to show all clips
Option-M	Add a marker and edit the marker's text
Control-1	Apply keyword 1 to the selection
Control-2	Apply keyword 2 to the selection
Control-3	Apply keyword 3 to the selection
Control-4	Apply keyword 4 to the selection
Control-5	Apply keyword 5 to the selection
Control-6	Apply keyword 6 to the selection
Control-7	Apply keyword 7 to the selection
Control-8	Apply keyword 8 to the selection
Control-9	Apply keyword 9 to the selection
Option-X	Clear the range selection
Option-O	Clear the range's end point
Option-I	Clear the range's start point
Control-M	Delete the selected marker
Control-Shift-M	Delete all of the markers in the selection

Keyboard Shortcut	Action
Command-Shift-A	Deselect all selected items
Control-Shift-C	Open the selected caption in the caption editor
F	Rate the browser selection as favorite
Control-F	Change the browser filter settings to show favorites
Control-H	Change the browser filter settings to hide rejected clips
Command-Shift-K	Create a new Keyword Collection
Command-Option-N	Create a new Smart Collection
R	Make the Range Selection tool active
Delete	Mark the current selection in the browser as rejected Note: The Delete key removes selected items if the timeline is active instead of the browser
Control-Delete	Change the browser filter settings to show rejected clips
Control-0	Remove all keywords from the browser selection
Option-Control-D	Apply Dialogue subroles to the selected clip's components
Option-Control-E	Apply Effects subroles to the selected clip's components
Option-Control-M	Apply Music subroles to the selected clip's components
Option-Control-T	Apply the Titles role to the selected clip
Option-Control-V	Apply the Video role to the selected clip
Command-A	Select all clips
X	Set the range selection to match the boundaries of the clip below the skimmer or playhead
Command-Shift-O	Set an additional range selection end point at the playhead or skimmer location
Command-Shift-I	Set an additional range selection start point at the playhead or skimmer location
O	Set the end point for the range
Control-O	Set the end point for the range while editing a text field
I	Set the start point for the range
Control-I	Set the start point for the range while editing a text field
U	Remove ratings from the selection

Organization

Keyboard Shortcut	Action
Option-N	Create a new event
Command-Shift-N	Create a new folder
Shift-F	Reveal the selected clip in the browser
Command-Option-Shift-F	Reveal the open project in the browser
Command-Option-G	Sync the selected event clips

Playback and Navigation

Keyboard Shortcut	Action
Shift-S	Turn audio skimming on or off
Command-Control-Y	Play the pick in context in the timeline
Command-Option-S	Turn clip skimming on or off
Option-Shift-3	Turn on audio-only mode for multicam cutting and switching
Option-Shift-1	Turn on audio/video mode for multicam cutting and switching
Option-Shift-2	Turn on video-only mode for multicam cutting and switching
Down Arrow	Go to the next item (in the browser) or the next edit point (in the timeline)
Control-Down Arrow	While editing a text field, go to the next item (in the browser) or the next edit point (in the timeline)
Shift-Left Arrow	Move the playhead back 10 frames
Shift-Right Arrow	Move the playhead forward 10 frames
Home key	Move the playhead to the beginning of the timeline or the first clip in the browser
End key	Move the playhead to the end of the timeline or to the last clip in the browser
Option-Shift-Apostrophe	Display the next bank of angles in the current multicam clip
Apostrophe	Move the playhead to the next edit point in the timeline
Option-Right Arrow	Move the playhead to the next field in an interlaced clip
Right Arrow	Move the playhead to the next frame
Option-Right Arrow	Move the playhead to the next audio subframe
Option-Shift-Semicolon	Display the previous bank of angles in the current multicam clip
Semicolon	Move the playhead to the previous edit point in the timeline

Keyboard Shortcut	Action
Option-Left Arrow	Move the playhead to the previous field in an interlaced clip
Left Arrow	Move the playhead to the previous frame
Option-Left Arrow	Move the playhead to the previous audio subframe
Shift-O	Move the playhead to the end of the range selection
Shift-I	Move the playhead to the beginning of the range selection
Command-Option-Control-Right Bracket	Roll the 360° viewer clockwise
Command-Option-Control-Left Bracket	Roll the 360° viewer counterclockwise
Command-Option-Control-Down Arrow	Tilt the 360° viewer down
Command-Option-Control-Left Arrow	Pan the 360° viewer to the left
Command-Option-Control-Right Arrow	Pan the 360° viewer to the right
Command-Option-Control-Up Arrow	Pan the 360° viewer up
Command-L	Turn looped playback on or off
Command-Option-Control-9	Mirror the display of the connected VR headset in the 360° viewer
Shift-A	Turn on or turn off audio monitoring for the angle being skimmed
Hyphen	Enter a negative timecode value to move the playhead back, move a clip earlier, or trim a range or clip, depending on your selection
Command-Control-Right Arrow	Go to the next item (in the browser) or the next edit point (in the timeline)
Control-Apostrophe	Move the playhead to the next marker
Command-Option-Control-7	Send 360° video to the connected VR headset
Shift-Question Mark	Play around the playhead position
L	Play forward (press L multiple times to increase the playback speed)
Option-Space Bar	Play from the playhead position
Command-Shift-F	Play full screen from the skimmer or playhead position
J	Play in reverse (press J multiple times to increase the reverse playback speed)
Control-J	Play in reverse while editing a text field (press J multiple times to increase the reverse playback speed)
Shift-Space Bar	Play in reverse
Forward Slash	Play the selection
Control-Shift-O	Play from the playhead to the end of the selection
Space Bar	Start or pause playback
Control-Space Bar	Start or pause playback while editing a text field

Keyboard Shortcut	Action
Equal Sign	Enter a positive timecode value to move the playhead forward, move a clip later, or trim a range or clip, depending on your selection
Command-Control-Left Arrow	Go to the previous item (in the browser) or the previous edit point (in the timeline)
Control-Semicolon	Move the playhead to the previous marker
Shift-V	Set the angle being skimmed as the monitoring angle
S	Turn skimming on or off
Option-Shift-A	Start or stop recording audio from the Record Voiceover window
K	Stop playback
Control-K	Stop playback while editing a text field
Command-Left Bracket	Go back one level in the timeline history
Command-Right Bracket	Go forward one level in the timeline history
Up Arrow	Go to the previous item (in the browser) or the previous edit point (in the timeline)
Control-Up Arrow	While editing a text field, go to the previous item (in the browser) or the previous edit point (in the timeline)

Share and Tools

Keyboard Shortcut	Action
Command-E	Share the selected project or clip using the default destination
A	Make the Select tool active
B	Make the Blade tool active
Shift-C	Make the Crop tool active and display onscreen controls for the selected clip or the topmost clip under the playhead
Option-D	Make the Distort tool active and display onscreen controls for the selected clip or the topmost clip under the playhead
H	Make the Hand tool active
P	Make the Position tool active
Shift-T	Make the Transform tool active and display onscreen controls for the selected clip or the topmost clip under the playhead
T	Make the Trim tool active
Z	Make the Zoom tool active

View

Keyboard Shortcut	Action
Option-Control-1	Display timeline clips with large audio waveforms only
Option-Control-2	Display timeline clips with large audio waveforms and small filmstrips
Option-Control-3	Display timeline clips with audio waveforms and video filmstrips of equal size
Option-Control-4	Display timeline clips with small audio waveforms and large filmstrips
Option-Control-6	Depending on the clip name setting, display timeline clips with clip names, role names, or active angle names only
Option-Control-5	Display timeline clips with large filmstrips only
Option-Control-Down Arrow	Decrease the size of audio waveforms for timeline clips
Option-Control-Up Arrow	Increase the size of audio waveforms for timeline clips
Command-Shift-Hyphen	Decrease the browser clip height
Command-Shift-Equal Sign	Increase the browser clip height
Command-Shift-Comma	Show fewer filmstrip frames in browser clips
Control-A	Show or hide the Audio Animation editor for the selected clips or components
Control-Y	Show or hide clip information when skimming in the browser
Control-V	Show or hide the Video Animation editor for the selected timeline clips
Command-Shift-Period	Show more filmstrip frames in browser clips
Command-Option-Shift-Comma	Show one frame per filmstrip
Command-Option-2	Switch the browser between filmstrip view and list view
Option-Shift-N	Show or hide clip names in the browser
Command-Plus Sign	Zoom in to the browser, viewer, or timeline
Command-Minus Sign	Zoom out of the browser, viewer, or timeline
Shift-Z	Zoom the contents to fit the size of the browser, viewer, or timeline
Control-Z	Turn zooming in to audio samples on or off

Windows

Keyboard Shortcut	Action
Command-1	Make the browser active
Command-Option-1	Show or hide the Titles and Generators sidebar

Keyboard Shortcut	Action
Command-Control-1	Show or hide the browser
Command-2	Make the timeline active
Command-Control-2	Show or hide the timeline
Command-Shift-2	Show or hide the timeline index for the open project
Command-3	Make the viewer active
Command-Control-3	Show or hide the event viewer
Command-4	Show or hide the inspector
Command-Option-4	Make the current inspector active
Command-Control-4	Switch between the half-height view and full-height view in the inspector
Command-5	Show or hide the Effects browser
Command-Control-5	Show or hide the Transitions browser
Command-6	Make the Color Board active
Command-Control-6	Show or hide the comparison viewer
Command-7	Show or hide the video scopes in the viewer
Command-Option-7	Show or hide the 360° viewer
Command-Shift-7	Show or hide the angle viewer
Command-8	Make the Audio Enhancements inspector active
Command-Option-8	Show or hide the Record Voiceover window
Command-Shift-8	Show or hide the audio meters
Command-9	Show or hide the Background Tasks window
Control-Tab	Go to the next pane in the inspector or the Color Board
Control-Shift-Tab	Go to the previous pane in the inspector or the Color Board
Command-Control-H	Show the histogram in the viewer
Command-Control-V	Show the vectorscope in the viewer
Command-Control-W	Show the waveform monitor in the viewer
Command-K	Show or hide the keyword editor
Command-1	Show or hide the Libraries sidebar
Command-Shift-1	Show or hide the Photos and Audio sidebar
Command-Grave Accent	Show or hide the sidebar

Logic Pro X
Version 10.5

General Keyboard Shortcuts

Keyboard Shortcut	Action
R	Record
Option-R	Record into cell
⠿ Asterisk	Record/Record Toggle
Command-Period	Discard Recording and Return to Last Play Position
Shift-R	Capture as Recording
⠿ Enter	Play
⠿ Period	Pause
⠿ 0	Stop
Space Bar	Play or Stop
Option-Underscore	Preview Selection-Based Processing
Comma	Rewind

LEARN BY KEY (Symbol ⠿)

Logic Pro comes with many preassigned keyboard shortcuts, but also has a powerful keyboard shortcut editor to create your own shortcuts. If you have a full-sized keyboard with a numeric keypad and you want to distinguish between number keys on the main keyboard area from the numeric keypad (numpad), press the Learn by Key Position button instead.

● Available when Advanced Tools are showing.

Keyboard Shortcut		Action
⠿ V		Forward
Shift-Comma		Fast Rewind
Shift-Period		Fast Forward
Control-Period		Forward by Transient
Control-Comma	ⓘ	Rewind by Transient
Shift-Enter		Play from Left Window Edge
⠿ Z		Go to Position
Command-Option-Control-I		Set Punch In Locator by Playhead
Command-Option-Control-Shift-I		Set Punch In Locator by Rounded Playhead
Command-Option-Control-O		Set Punch Out Locator by Playhead
Command-Option-Control-Shift-O		Set Punch Out Locator Point by Rounded Playhead
Command-U	ⓘ	Set Locators by Regions/Events/Marquee and Enable Cycle
U		Set Rounded Locators by Regions/Events and Enable Cycle
Shift-Space Bar		Play from Selection
⠿ Equal Sign		Swap Left and Right Locator
Command-Shift-Period		Move Locators Forward by Cycle Length
Command-Shift-Comma	ⓘ	Move Locators Backwards by Cycle Length
Control-Home	ⓘ	Go to Selection Start
Control-End		Go to Selection End
Option-Return		Go to End of Last Region
Return		Go to Beginning
Option-Apostrophe		Create Marker
Option-Control-Apostrophe		Create Marker Without Rounding
Option-Shift-Apostrophe		Create Marker for Selected Regions
Option-Delete		Delete Marker
Option-Control-C		Set Locators by Marker and Enable Cycle
Option-Control-Comma		Set Locators by Previous Marker and Enable Cycle
Option-Control-Period		Set Locators by Next Marker and Enable Cycle
Option-Comma		Go to Previous Marker and Set Locators
Option-Period		Go to Next Marker and Set Locators

ⓘ Available when Advanced Tools are showing.

Keyboard Shortcut	Action
Option-Forward Slash	Go to Marker Number
Shift-Apostrophe	Rename Marker
⠿ 1	Go to Marker Number 1
⠿ 2	Go to Marker Number 2
⠿ 3	Go to Marker Number 3
⠿ 4	Go to Marker Number 4
⠿ 5	Go to Marker Number 5
⠿ 6	Go to Marker Number 6
⠿ 7	Go to Marker Number 7
⠿ 8	Go to Marker Number 8
⠿ 9	Go to Marker Number 9
⠿ Control-0	Go to Marker Number 10
⠿ Control-1	Go to Marker Number 11
⠿ Control-2	Go to Marker Number 12
⠿ Control-3	Go to Marker Number 13
⠿ Control-4	Go to Marker Number 14
⠿ Control-5	Go to Marker Number 15
⠿ Control-6	Go to Marker Number 16
⠿ Control-7	Go to Marker Number 17
⠿ Control-8	Go to Marker Number 18
⠿ Control-9	Go to Marker Number 19
C	Cycle Mode
Command-Option-Shift-Period	Double Cycle/Loop Length
Command-Option-Shift-Comma	Halve Cycle/Loop Length
Command-Option-Control-P ⓘ	Autopunch Mode
⠿ Forward Slash	Replace
Control-S	Solo Mode
Option-S	Set Solo Lock Mode
Option-Shift-S	Reselect Solo-Locked Regions

ⓘ Available when Advanced Tools are showing.

Keyboard Shortcut		Action
Command-Option-Control-S		Clear/Recall Solo
Control-Shift-M		Mute Off for all
Control-C		Cycle Audition on or off
K		MIDI/Monitor Metronome Click
Shift-K		Count In
⠿ 1	🛈	Recall Screenset 1
⠿ 2	🛈	Recall Screenset 2
⠿ 3	🛈	Recall Screenset 3
⠿ 4	🛈	Recall Screenset 4
⠿ 5	🛈	Recall Screenset 5
⠿ 6	🛈	Recall Screenset 6
⠿ 7	🛈	Recall Screenset 7
⠿ 8	🛈	Recall Screenset 8
⠿ 9	🛈	Recall Screenset 9
⠿ Control-1	🛈	Recall Screenset 1x
⠿ Control-2	🛈	Recall Screenset 2x
⠿ Control-3	🛈	Recall Screenset 3x
⠿ Control-4	🛈	Recall Screenset 4x
⠿ Control-5	🛈	Recall Screenset 5x
⠿ Control-6	🛈	Recall Screenset 6x
⠿ Control-7	🛈	Recall Screenset 7x
⠿ Control-8	🛈	Recall Screenset 8x
⠿ Control-9	🛈	Recall Screenset 9x
Option-Shift-R		Region Inspector Float
Command-Comma		Open the preferences window
Option-A	🛈	Open Automation Preferences...
Command-1		Open Main Window...
Command-2	🛈	Open Mixer...
Command-3	🛈	Open Smart Controls

🛈 Available when Advanced Tools are showing.

Keyboard Shortcut		Action
Command-4		Open Piano Roll
Command-5		Open Score Editor
Command-6		Open Audio File Editor
Command-7		Open Event List...
Command-8		Open Project Audio
Command-9		Open Transform
Command-0		Open Environment
Option-Control-Return		Note Repeat
Option-Control-Delete		Spot Erase
Command-K		Show or hide Musical Typing
Option-E		Show or hide Event Float
X		Show or hide Mixer
B		Show or hide Smart Controls
N		Show or hide Score Editor
Option-Control-Shift-S		Show or hide Staff Style Window
Option-Control-Shift-I		Show or hide Score Sets Window
P		Show or hide Piano Roll
Command-Option-K		Show or hide Step Input Keyboard
O		Show or hide Loop Browser
Y		Show or hide Library
W		Show or hide Audio File Editor
Shift-Forward Slash		Show or hide Quick Help
Command-Forward Slash		Show Detailed Help
Shift-W		Open in External Sample Editor
Option-Shift-T		Open Tempo List
Option-K		Open Key Commands
Option-C		Show or hide Colors
Command-Control-F		Enter/Exit Full Screen
Command-Option-O		Open Movie
Command-Control-O		Toggle Current Track Automation Off/Read

Available when Advanced Tools are showing.

Keyboard Shortcut		Action
Command-Control-A		Toggle Current Track Automation Latch/Read
Command-Control-Shift-O		Set All Tracks to Automation Off
Command-Control-Shift-R		Set All Tracks to Automation Read
Command-Control-Shift-T		Set All Tracks to Automation Touch
Command-Control-Shift-L		Set All Tracks to Automation Latch
Command-Control-E		Track Automation Event List
Command-Option-Control-A	⊕	Toggle Automation Quick Access
Shift-G	⊕	Enable/Disable Automation Groups
Option-Shift-G	⊕	Open Group Settings
Command-W		Close the frontmost window
Command-Grave Accent		Cycle Through Windows
Command-Shift-Grave Accent		Cycle Through Windows (counter clockwise)
Up Arrow		Select Previous Track
Down Arrow		Select Next Track
Command-Shift-N	⊕	New Empty Project
Command-N		New from Template
Command-O		Open
Option-P		Project Settings
Command-Option-W		Close Project
Command-S		Save the document
Command-Shift-S		Save Project as
Command-P		Print the document
Command-I	⊕	Import
Command-Option-E		Export Selection as MIDI File
Command-E	⊕	Export Track as Audio File
Command-Shift-E	⊕	Export All Tracks as Audio Files
Command-Option-M		Zoom Window
Command-Shift-I		Import Audio File
Shift-Right Bracket		Next Channel Strip Setting of Focused Track
Shift-Left Bracket		Previous Channel Strip Setting of Focused Track

⊕ Available when Advanced Tools are showing.

Keyboard Shortcut	Action
Command-Option-C	Copy Channel Strip Setting
Command-Option-V	Paste Channel Strip Setting
Right Bracket	Next Patch, Plug-in Setting or Sampler Instrument
Left Bracket	Previous Patch, Plug-in Setting or Sampler Instrument
M	Toggle Channel Strip Mute
S	Toggle Channel Strip Solo
Control-I	Toggle Channel Strip Input Monitoring
Control-Shift-S	Toggle Channel Strip Format (mono/stereo)
V	Show or hide All Plug-in Windows
Option-Control-M	Set Nudge Value to Bar
Option-Control-B	Set Nudge Value to Beat
Option-Control-D	Set Nudge Value to Division
Option-Control-T	Set Nudge Value to Tick
Option-Control-F	Set Nudge Value to SMPTE Frame
Option-Control-H	Set Nudge Value to 0.5 SMPTE Frame
Option-Control-S	Set Nudge Value to Sample
Option-Control-1	Set Nudge Value to 1 ms
Option-Control-0	Set Nudge Value to 10 ms

Global Control Surfaces Commands

Keyboard Shortcut		Action
Option-Shift-K	ⓘ	Open Controller Assignments
Command-L	ⓘ	Learn new Controller Assignment

ⓘ Available when Advanced Tools are showing.

Various Windows

Keyboard Shortcut	Action
Command-Z	Undo the previous command
Command-Shift-Z	Redo, revoking the undo command
Command-Option-Z ⓘ	Undo History
Command-X	Cut the selected text or item and copy it to the clipboard
Command-C	Copy the selected text or item to the clipboard
Command-V	Paste the contents of the clipboard
Command-A	Select all items
T	Show Tool Menu
Option-Page Down	Set Next Tool
Option-Page Up	Set Previous Tool
Page Up	Page Up
Page Down	Page Down
Home	Page Left
End	Page Right
Option-Shift-I	Show or hide Local Inspector
Option-O	MIDI Out Toggle
Option-I	MIDI In Toggle
⠿ Right Bracket	Increase Last Clicked Parameter by 1
⠿ Left Bracket	Decrease Last Clicked Parameter by 1
⠿ Shift-Right Bracket	Increase Last Clicked Parameter by 10
⠿ Shift-Left Bracket	Decrease Last Clicked Parameter by 10

Windows Showing Audio Files

Keyboard Shortcut	Action
Command-Shift-R	Show File(s) in Finder
⠿ Control-0	Snap Edits to Zero Crossings
Command-Semicolon	Add to Tracks

ⓘ Available when Advanced Tools are showing.

Keyboard Shortcut	Action
Option-Space Bar	Preview
Option-Shift-P	Show or hide Selection-based Processing
Option-Control-P	Apply Selection-based Processing Again

Main Window Tracks and Various Editors

Keyboard Shortcut		Action
Command-Option-N		New Tracks
Command-Option-A		New Audio Track
Command-Option-S		New Software Instrument Track
Command-Option-U		New Drummer Track
Command-Option-X		New External MIDI Track
Command-D		New Track with Duplicate Setting
Control-Return		New Track with Next Channel/MIDI Channel
Control-Shift-Return		New Track with Same Channel Strip/Instrument
Command-Delete		Delete Track
Command-Option-Delete		Delete Unused Tracks
Shift-D	⊕	Deselect All
Shift-I	⊕	Invert Selection
Shift-F	⊕	Select All Following
Control-Shift-F	⊕	Select All Following of Same Track/Pitch
Shift-L	⊕	Select All Inside Locators
Shift-O	⊕	Select Overlapped Regions/Events
Shift-E	⊕	Select Equal Regions/Events
Shift-S	⊕	Select Similar Regions/Events
Shift-P	⊕	Select Same Subpositions
Shift-M	⊕	Select Muted Regions/Events
Shift-C	⊕	Select Same-Color Regions/Events
Shift-Home		Select First, or Shift Marquee Selection Left

⊕ Available when Advanced Tools are showing.

Keyboard Shortcut		Action
Shift-End		Select Last, or Shift Marquee Selection Right
Left Arrow		Select Previous Region/Event or Move Marquee End (or Marquee Point) to Previous Transient
Right Arrow		Select Next Region/Event or Move Marquee End (or Marquee Point) to Next Transient
Shift-Left Arrow		Toggle Previous Region/Event or Move Marquee Start (or Extend Marquee Selection) to Previous Transient
Shift-Right Arrow		Toggle Next Region/Event or Move Marquee Start (or Extend Marquee Selection) to Next Transient
Shift-Grave Accent		Scroll to Selection
L		Loop Regions/Folders On or off
Q		Quantize Selected Events
Command-Option-Q		Undo Quantization
Option-D	🔵	Delete Duplicated Events
Command-Shift-V	🔵	Paste Replace
Command-R		Repeat Regions/Events
Command-J		Join Regions/Notes
Command-Control-T		Split Regions/Events at Locators or Marquee Selection
Command-T		Split Regions/Events at Playhead Position
Semicolon	🔵	Move Region/Event to Playhead Position (Pickup Clock)
Shift-Semicolon	🔵	Move Region/Event to Playhead Position and Select Next Region/Event (Pickup Clock+)
Command-Left Bracket	🔵	Set Region/Event/Marquee Start to Playhead Position
Command-Right Bracket	🔵	Set Region/Event/Marquee End to Playhead Position
Option-Control-Right Arrow	🔵	Nudge Region/Event Position Right by Nudge Value
Option-Control-Left Arrow	🔵	Nudge Region/Event Position Left by Nudge Value
Option-Shift-Right Arrow	🔵	Nudge Region/Event Length Right by Nudge Value
Option-Shift-Left Arrow	🔵	Nudge Region/Event Length Left by Nudge Value
Command-Option-Control-Right Arrow	🔵	Rotate Right by Nudge Value
Command-Option-Control-Left Arrow	🔵	Rotate Left by Nudge Value
Command-Control-Right Arrow		Open Track Stack
Command-Control-Left Arrow		Close Track Stack

🔵 Available when Advanced Tools are showing.

Keyboard Shortcut		Action
Control-M		Mute Notes/Regions/Folders On or off
Command-G		Snap to Grid On or off
Option-Left Bracket	ⓘ	Shuffle Left
Option-Right Bracket	ⓘ	Shuffle Right
Option-L		Show or hide Live Loops
Option-N		Show or hide Tracks area
Command-B		Bounce

Live Loops Grid

Keyboard Shortcut	Action
Return	Play Live Loops (Play Queued Cells or Selected Cells/Scene
Down Arrow	Select Next Lower Cell, or Next Track
Up Arrow	Select Next Upper Cell, or Previous Track
Shift-Up Arrow	Extend Cell, or Track Selection Up
Shift-Down Arrow	Extend Cell, or Track Selection Down
Command-Return	Stop All Cells
Option-Return	Queue Cell Playback
Option-Left Arrow	Focus Previous Scene
Option-Right Arrow	Focus Next Scene
Command-Home	Copy to Live Loops
Command-End	Insert Scene(s) at Playhead

Various Editors

Keyboard Shortcut		Action
Shift-H	ⓘ	Select Same Channels
Shift-A		Select Same Articulation IDs
Backslash	ⓘ	Trim Note to Remove Overlaps for Adjacent

ⓘ Available when Advanced Tools are showing.

Keyboard Shortcut		Action
Shift-Backslash	ⓘ	Trim Note End to Following Notes (Force Legato)
Shift-Up Arrow	ⓘ	Select Highest Notes
Shift-Down Arrow	ⓘ	Select Lowest Notes
Option-Up Arrow	ⓘ	Transpose Event +1 Semitone
Option-Down Arrow	ⓘ	Transpose Event -1 Semitone
Option-Shift-Up Arrow	ⓘ	Transpose Event +12 Semitones
Option-Shift-Down Arrow	ⓘ	Transpose Event -12 Semitones
Option-Control-R		Show Event Position and Length as Time or Bars/Beats

Time Ruler

Keyboard Shortcut		Action
Grave Accent		Catch Playhead Position
Command-Option-Control-R		Secondary Ruler
Control-G	ⓘ	Grid
Control-Grave Accent		Scroll in Play
G		Show or hide Global Tracks
Option-G	ⓘ	Configure Global Tracks
Command-Shift-A		Show or hide Arrangement Track
Command-Shift-K	ⓘ	Show or hide Marker Track
Command-Shift-O		Show or hide Movie Track
Command-Shift-X		Show or hide Transposition Track
Command-Shift-T		Show or hide Tempo Track
Command-Shift-B	ⓘ	Show or hide Beat Mapping Track
Apostrophe	ⓘ	Show or hide Marker Track Only
Command-Left Arrow		Zoom Horizontal Out
Command-Right Arrow		Zoom Horizontal In
Command-Up Arrow		Zoom Vertical Out
Command-Down Arrow		Zoom Vertical In

ⓘ Available when Advanced Tools are showing.

Keyboard Shortcut	Action
Command-Option-Control-1	Recall Zoom 1
Command-Option-Control-2	Recall Zoom 2
Command-Option-Control-3	Recall Zoom 3
Command-Option-Control-Shift-1	Save as Zoom 1
Command-Option-Control-Shift-2	Save as Zoom 2
Command-Option-Control-Shift-3	Save as Zoom 3
Control-Shift-Z	Zoom to Fit Locators, Store Navigation Snapshot
Z	Toggle Zoom to Fit Selection or All Contents
Shift-Z	Store Navigation Snapshot
Option-Z	Navigation: Back
Option-Shift-Z	Navigation: Forward
Control-M	Mute Notes/Regions/Folders On or off
Command-Shift-Y	Region Automation: Disable
Command-Y	Automation: Autodefine

Main Window Tracks

Keyboard Shortcut		Action
Shift-Up Arrow		Extend Track Selection Up
Shift-Down Arrow		Extend Track Selection Down
Left Arrow		Select Previous Region on Selected Track
Right Arrow		Select Next Region on Selected Track
Command-Control-Shift-1	⊕	Create 1 Automation Point at Region Borders
Command-Control-Shift-2	⊕	Create 2 Automation Points at Region Borders
Command-Control-1	⊕	Create 1 Automation Point at Every Region Border
Command-Control-2	⊕	Create 2 Automation Points at Every Region Border
Control-Delete	⊕	Delete Redundant Automation Points
Command-Control-Delete	⊕	Delete Visible Automation on Selected Track
Command-Control-Shift-Delete		Delete All Automation on Selected Track

⊕ Available when Advanced Tools are showing.

Keyboard Shortcut		Action
Control-Shift-Delete		Delete Orphaned Automation on Selected Track
Command-Control-Up Arrow		Move Visible Region Data to Track Automation
Command-Control-Down Arrow		Move Visible Track Automation to Region
Command-Control-Shift-Up Arrow		Move All Region Data to Track Automation
Command-Control-Shift-Down Arrow		Move All Track Automation to Region
Command-Control-F		Pack Take Folder
Command-Control-U		Unpack Take Folder to Existing Tracks
Command-Control-Shift-U		Unpack Take Folder to New Tracks
Option-F		Un/disclose Take Folder
Option-Shift-U		Flatten Take Folder
Option-U		Flatten and Merge Take Folder
Shift-T		Rename Take or Comp
Option-Shift-Delete		Delete Take or Comp
Option-Q		Toggle Take Folder Quick Swipe Comping Mode
Command-Shift-Up Arrow		Select Previous Take or Comp
Command-Shift-Down Arrow		Select Next Take or Comp
Command-Shift-D		Create Track Stack
Command-Shift-F		Create Folder Stack
Command-Shift-G		Create Summing Stack
Command-Shift-U		Flatten Stack
Control-B		Bounce Regions in Place
Command-Control-B		Bounce Tracks in Place
Control-D		Drum Replacement/Doubling
H		Toggle Hide View
Control-H		Hide/Show Current Track and Select Next Track
Control-Shift-H		Unhide All Tracks
Control-Shift-1		Toggle Hide Group 1
Control-Shift-2		Toggle Hide Group 2
Control-Shift-3		Toggle Hide Group 3
Control-Shift-4		Toggle Hide Group 4

Available when Advanced Tools are showing.

Keyboard Shortcut		Action
Control-Shift-5	ⓘ	Toggle Hide Group 5
Control-Shift-6	ⓘ	Toggle Hide Group 6
Control-Shift-7	ⓘ	Toggle Hide Group 7
Control-Shift-8	ⓘ	Toggle Hide Group 8
Control-Shift-9	ⓘ	Toggle Hide Group 9
Option-M		Toggle Track On
Control-R		Toggle Track Record Enable
Command-Option-Control-Down Arrow	ⓘ	Individual Track Zoom In
Command-Option-Control-Up Arrow	ⓘ	Individual Track Zoom Out
Command-Option-Control-Z	ⓘ	Toggle Individual Track Zoom
Control-Z		Toggle Zoom Focused Track
Command-Option-Control-Delete	ⓘ	Reset Individual Track Zoom
Option-Control-Delete	ⓘ	Individual Track Zoom Reset for All Tracks
Option-X		Audio Crossfade Options for Merge
J	ⓘ	Join Regions per Tracks
Option-Control-X		Apply Default Crossfade
Option-Shift-X		Apply Last Edited Fade Again
Control-A		Convert Alias to a Region Copy
Option-Shift-A		Select All Aliases of Region
Command-Control-X	ⓘ	Cut Section Between Locators (Global)
Command-Control-Z	ⓘ	Insert Silence Between Locators (Global)
Command-Control-V	ⓘ	Insert Snipped Section at Playhead (Global)
Command-Control-R	ⓘ	Repeat Section Between Locators (Global)
Shift-Return		Rename Track
Control-Shift-T	ⓘ	Move Selected Regions to Selected Track
Command-Option-Shift-R	ⓘ	Move Region to Recorded Position
Option-Control-Shift-T	ⓘ	Copy Selected Regions to Selected Track
Command-Option-R	ⓘ	Convert Regions to New Regions
Command-Option-F	ⓘ	Convert Regions to New Audio Files
Control-E	ⓘ	Convert Regions to New Sampler Track

ⓘ Available when Advanced Tools are showing.

Logic Pro X | 165

Keyboard Shortcut		Action
Command-Option-L	ⓘ	Time Stretch Region Length to Locators
Command-Option-B	ⓘ	Time Stretch Region Length to Nearest Bar
Command-Option-T		Detect Tempo of Selected Region...
Control-X		Remove Silence from Audio Region...
Control-Shift-O		Add Region to Loop Library
Control-N	ⓘ	Normalize Region Parameters
Control-Q	ⓘ	Apply Quantization Destructively
Control-L	ⓘ	Convert Loops to Regions
Control-Backslash		Set Optimal Region Sizes Rounded by Bar
Backslash	ⓘ	Remove Overlaps
Shift-Backslash	ⓘ	Trim Region End to Next Region
Option-Backslash	ⓘ	Trim Regions to Fill within Locators
Command-Backslash	ⓘ	Crop Regions outside Locators or Marquee Selection
A		Hide/Show Track Automation
Command-F		Hide/Show Flex Pitch/Time
Control-Shift-Left Bracket	ⓘ	Trim Region Start to Previous Transient
Control-Shift-Right Bracket	ⓘ	Trim Region Start to Next Transient
Control-Left Bracket	ⓘ	Trim Region End to Previous Transient
Control-Right Bracket	ⓘ	Trim Region End to Next Transient
Shift-N		Rename Regions
Option-Shift-N		Name Regions by Track Name
Command-Option-Shift-N		Name Tracks by Region Name
Option-Shift-C		Color Regions by Track Color
Command-Option-Shift-C	ⓘ	Color Tracks by Region Color
Command-Hyphen	ⓘ	Waveform Vertical Zoom Out
Command-Equal Sign	ⓘ	Waveform Vertical Zoom In
Command-Option-Control-T	ⓘ	Show or hide Toolbar
Option-T	ⓘ	Configure Track Header
E		Show or hide Editor
Option-N		Show or hide Note Pad

ⓘ Available when Advanced Tools are showing.

Keyboard Shortcut	Action
D ⓘ	Show or hide List Editors
F	Show or hide Browsers
Command-Shift-M	Show or hide Output Track
Command-Option-G	Alignment Guides On or off
Command-Option-Control-N	New Track Alternative
Command-Option-Control-D	Duplicate Track Alternative
Command-Option-Control-Delete	Delete Inactive Track Alternatives
Command-Option-Control-Return	Rename Track Alternative
Option-Control-A	Show or hide Inactive Track Alternatives
Option-Control-Up Arrow	Activate Next Track Alternative
Option-Control-Down Arrow	Activate Previous Track Alternative
Option-L	Show Live Loops Grid Only
Option-N	Show Tracks Area Only

Mixer

Keyboard Shortcut	Action
Shift-X ⓘ	Cycle Through Mixer Modes (Single, Arrange, All)
Option-Shift-D	Deselect All
Shift-A	Select Audio Channel Strips
Shift-S	Select Instrument Channel Strips
Shift-F	Select Auxiliary Channel Strips
Shift-O	Select Output Channel Strips
Shift-E	Select MIDI Channel Strips
Shift-C	Select Same-Color Channel Strips
Shift-M	Select Muted Channel Strips
Left Arrow	Select Previous (Left) Channel Strip
Right Arrow	Select Next (Right) Channel Strip
Control-N	Create New Auxiliary Channel Strip

ⓘ Available when Advanced Tools are showing.

Keyboard Shortcut	Action
Control-T	Create Tracks for Selected Channel Strips
Option-X	Configure Channel Strip Components

MIDI Environment

Keyboard Shortcut		Action
Control-Delete	⊕	Clear Cables only
Option-Left Arrow	⊕	Object move left
Option-Right Arrow	⊕	Object move right
Option-Up Arrow	⊕	Object move up
Option-Down Arrow	⊕	Object move down
Option-Shift-Left Arrow	⊕	Object Width -1 Pixel
Option-Shift-Right Arrow	⊕	Object Width +1 Pixel
Option-Shift-Up Arrow	⊕	Object Height -1 Pixel
Option-Shift-Down Arrow	⊕	Object Height +1 Pixel
Control-C	⊕	Show or hide Cables
Control-P	⊕	Protect Cabling/Positions
Shift-I	⊕	Invert Selection
Shift-U	⊕	Select Unused Instruments
Shift-Right Arrow	⊕	Select Cable Destination
Shift-Left Arrow	⊕	Select Cable Origin
Control-V	⊕	Send Selected Fader Values
Command-Delete	⊕	Delete Layer
Control-S	⊕	Cable serially

⊕ Available when Advanced Tools are showing.

Piano Roll

Keyboard Shortcut		Action
Shift-T	⊙	Toggle Time Handles
Control-Shift-B		Define Brush Pattern & Set Brush Tool
Control-Shift-Delete		Reset Brush Pattern

Score Editor

Keyboard Shortcut		Action
Control-P	⊙	Page View
Control-F	⊙	Explode Folders
Control-X	⊙	Explode Polyphony
Control-Shift-N	⊙	Hide/Show Instrument Names
Control-Shift-R	⊙	Hide/Show Page Rulers
Control-Forward Slash	⊙	Go to Page
Command-Option-Shift-V	⊙	Paste Multiple
Left Arrow		Select Next Event
Right Arrow		Select Previous Event
Down Arrow		Next Staff
Up Arrow		Previous Staff
Control-Shift-I	⊙	Force Interpretation
Control-I	⊙	Defeat Interpretation
Option-Control-Up Arrow	⊙	Stems: Up
Option-Control-Down Arrow	⊙	Stems: Down
Command-Option-Up Arrow	⊙	Stem End: Move Up
Command-Option-Down Arrow	⊙	Stem End: Move Down
Option-Control-Shift-Up Arrow	⊙	Ties: Up
Option-Control-Shift-Down Arrow	⊙	Ties: Down
Control-B	⊙	Beam Selected Notes
Control-U	⊙	Unbeam Selected Notes

⊙ Available when Advanced Tools are showing.

Keyboard Shortcut		Action
Control-D	ⓘ	Default Beams
Shift-3	ⓘ	Enharmonic Shift: #
Shift-B	ⓘ	Enharmonic Shift: b
Control-Shift-Delete	ⓘ	Reset Note Attributes
Control-Shift-C	ⓘ	Assign MIDI Channels Based on Score Split
Command-Option-Control-Up Arrow		Nudge Position Up
Command-Option-Control-Down Arrow		Nudge Position Down
Command-Option-Control-Left Arrow		Nudge Position Left
Command-Option-Control-Right Arrow		Nudge Position Right
Option-Control-Shift-F	ⓘ	Settings: Global Format
Option-Control-Shift-N	ⓘ	Settings: Numbers and Names
Option-Control-Shift-G	ⓘ	Settings: Guitar Tablature
Option-Control-Shift-C	ⓘ	Settings: Chords and Grids
Option-Control-Shift-L	ⓘ	Settings: Clefs and Signatures
Option-Control-Shift-X	ⓘ	Settings: Extended Layout
Option-Control-Shift-M	ⓘ	Settings: MIDI Meaning
Option-Control-Shift-O	ⓘ	Settings: Score Color
Control-Shift-Comma		Insert: Crescendo.
Control-Shift-Period		Insert: Decrescendo
Option-Control-Shift-Delete		Clear Main Finger
Option-Control-Shift-1		Set Main Finger 1
Option-Control-Shift-2		Set Main Finger 2
Option-Control-Shift-3		Set Main Finger 3
Option-Control-Shift-4		Set Main Finger 4
Option-Control-Shift-5		Set Main Finger 5

ⓘ Available when Advanced Tools are showing.

Event Editor

Keyboard Shortcut		Action
Up Arrow		Select Previous Event
Down Arrow		Select Next Event
Control-Shift-A	ⓘ	Length as Absolute Position
Control-Shift-D		Articulation ID
Control-Shift-R	ⓘ	Relative Position
Command-D		Duplicate Event and Numerical Edit
Shift-V		Copy Value to All Following Events

Step Editor

Keyboard Shortcut		Action
Command-Option-N	ⓘ	Create Lane
Command-Delete	ⓘ	Delete Lane
Control-C	ⓘ	Copy Lane
Control-V	ⓘ	Paste Lane
Control-A		Toggle Auto Define
Down Arrow		Select Next Lane
Up Arrow		Select Previous Lane

Step Sequencer

Keyboard Shortcut	Action
Command-R	Repeat Step
Command-Option-Control-V	Paste Steps
Option-Control-V	Paste Row Settings
Command-Delete	Delete Row
Command-Shift-R	Randomize Current Edit Mode Values for All Rows
Control-E	Show or hide All Edit Mode values

ⓘ Available when Advanced Tools are showing.

Keyboard Shortcut	Action
Command-Shift-P	Save Pattern
Command-Shift-T	Save Template
Command-D	Duplicate Row
Command-L	Learn Mode
Up Arrow	Select Step Above
Down Arrow	Select Step Below
Right Arrow	Select Previous Step
Left Arrow	Select Next Step
Command-Option-Control-Right Arrow	Pattern Rotate Right
Command-Option-Control-Left Arrow	Pattern Rotate Left
Option-Underscore	Preview

Project Audio

Keyboard Shortcut		Action
Up Arrow	🛈	Select Previous Audio File
Down Arrow	🛈	Select Next Audio File
Shift-Return	🛈	Rename
Control-F	🛈	Add Audio File
Control-R	🛈	Add Region
Command-Delete	🛈	Delete File(s)
Control-O	🛈	Optimize File(s)
Control-B	🛈	Backup File(s)
Control-K	🛈	Copy/Convert File(s)
Shift-U	🛈	Select Unused
Option-Down Arrow	🛈	Show All Regions
Option-Up Arrow	🛈	Hide All Regions
Control-X	🛈	Remove Silence from Audio Region
Control-I	🛈	Import Region Information

🛈 Available when Advanced Tools are showing.

Keyboard Shortcut		Action
Control-E		Export Region Information
Control-G		Create Group

Audio File Editor

Keyboard Shortcut		Action
Command-Option-Control-Space Bar		Play/Stop All
Option-Control-Shift-Space Bar		Play/Stop Region
Option-Control-Space Bar		Play/Stop Region from Anchor
Control-B		Create Backup
Command-Option-Control-B		Revert to Backup
Command-Option-S		Save Selection As...
Page Up		Region > Selection
Page Down		Selection > Region
Control-Home		Go to Selection Start
Control-End		Go to Selection End
Option-Control-Left Arrow		Go to Region Start
Option-Control-Right Arrow		Go to Region End
Option-Control-Down Arrow		Go to Region Anchor
Option-Left Arrow		Go to Previous Transient
Option-Right Arrow		Go to Next Transient
Shift-Left Arrow		Set Selection Start to Previous Transient
Shift-Right Arrow		Set Selection Start to Next Transient
Left Arrow		Set Selection End to Previous Transient
Right Arrow		Set Selection End to Next Transient
Command-Shift-Left Arrow		Selection Start and End to Previous Transient
Command-Shift-Right Arrow		Selection Start and End to Next Transient
Command-Option-Left Arrow		Selection Start and End to Previous Transient and Play
Command-Option-Right Arrow		Selection Start and End to Next Transient and Play

ⓘ Available when Advanced Tools are showing.

Keyboard Shortcut		Action
Control-T	ⓘ	Toggle Transient Editing Mode
Control-Equal Sign	ⓘ	Increase Number of Transients
Control-Hyphen	ⓘ	Decrease Number of Transients
Option-Control-Shift-Left Arrow	ⓘ	Select All Previous
Option-Control-Shift-Right Arrow	ⓘ	Select All Following
Control-R	ⓘ	Create New Region
Control-N	ⓘ	Normalize
Control-G	ⓘ	Change Gain
Control-I	ⓘ	Fade In
Control-O	ⓘ	Fade Out
Control-Delete	ⓘ	Silence
Control-Shift-I	ⓘ	Invert
Control-Shift-R	ⓘ	Reverse
Control-Shift-T	ⓘ	Trim
Control-D	ⓘ	Remove DC Offset
Control-P	ⓘ	Time and Pitch Machine
Shift-P	ⓘ	Search Peak
Shift-S	ⓘ	Search Silence
Control-A	ⓘ	Lock Position in Track when Moving Anchor

Smart Tempo Editor

Keyboard Shortcut	Action
T	Tap Tempo
D	Tap Tempo (Downbeat)
M	Toggle Metronome
Left Arrow	Scroll Left
Right Arrow	Scroll Right
Shift-Left Arrow	Select from Start to Cursor

ⓘ Available when Advanced Tools are showing.

Keyboard Shortcut	Action
Shift-Right Arrow	Select from Cursor to End
Up Arrow	Zoom All
Down Arrow	Center around Cursor

Sampler

Keyboard Shortcut	Action
Shift-I	Invert Selection
Control-F	Load Audio Sample
Control-Z	New Zone
Control-G	New Group
Command-Option-Shift-S	Export Sampler Instrument and Sample Files
Option-Left Arrow	Shift Selected Zone(s)/Group(s) Left
Option-Right Arrow	Shift Selected Zone(s)/Group(s) Right
Option-Shift-Left Arrow	Shift Selected Zone(s)/Group(s) Left (Zones incl. Root Key)
Option-Shift-Right Arrow	Shift Selected Zone(s)/Group(s) Right (Zones incl. Root Key)
Command-Option-S	Save Instrument
Control-O	Load Multiple Samples
Control-W	Open in Audio File Editor

Step Input Keyboard

Keyboard Shortcut	Action
A	Note 'C'
W	Note 'C#'
S	Note 'D'
E	Note 'D#'
D	Note 'E'
F	Note 'F'
T	Note 'F#'
G	Note 'G'

Keyboard Shortcut	Action
Y	Note 'G#'
H	Note 'A'
U	Note 'A#'
J	Note 'B'
Space Bar	Rest
Shift-3	Next note will be sharp.
Shift-B	Next note will be flat.
Grave Accent	Chord Mode
Control-Delete	Delete
Left Arrow	Step Backward.
Right Arrow	Step Forward.
Shift-Z	Octave - 2
Z	Octave - 1
X	Octave + 1
Shift-X	Octave + 2
1	1/1 Note
2	1/2 Note
3	1/4 Note
4	1/8 Note
5	1/16 Note
6	1/32 Note
7	1/64 Note
8	1/128 Note
9	Triplets on or off
0	Dotted Note Values On or off.
C	Velocity 16 (ppp)
V	Velocity 32 (pp)
B	Velocity 48 (p)
N	Velocity 64 (mp)
M	Velocity 80 (mf)
Comma	Velocity 96 (f)

Keyboard Shortcut	Action
Period	Velocity 112 (ff)
Forward Slash	Velocity 127 (fff)
Hyphen	Sustain inserted note(s)
Q	Quantize note starts on or off

Tools

Keyboard Shortcut	Action
I	Scissors tool
G	Glue tool
E	Eraser tool
Shift-M	MIDI Thru tool
Shift-T	Text tool
S	Solo tool
P	Pencil tool
H	Crosshair tool
M	Mute tool
F	Finger tool
L	Layout tool
Y	Zoom tool
Z	Resize tool
J	Voice Separation tool
C	Camera tool
V	Velocity tool
Q	Quantize tool
A	Fade tool
U	Automation Select tool
W	Automation Curve tool
R	Marquee tool
X	Flex tool
B	Brush tool

MainStage 3

Version 3.4.4

Concerts and Layouts

Keyboard Shortcut	Action
Command-N	New concert
Command-O	Open concert
Command-W	Close concert, or close the active plug-in window
Command-S	Save concert
Command-Shift-S	Save concert as
Command-Control-O	Import layout
Command-Control-Shift-S	Export layout

Patches and Sets

Keyboard Shortcut	Action
Command-Option-N	Add a new patch
Command-Option-S	Add a new set
Command-I	Import patches or sets
Command-E	Export patch, export set, or export as set
Command-Up Arrow	Select the previous patch
Command-Down Arrow	Select the next patch
Command-Left Arrow	Select the first patch in the previous set
Command-Right Arrow	Select the first patch in the next set
Command-Option-Shift-S	Create a new set from selected patches

Keyboard Shortcut	Action
Option-Shift-M	Move the selected patch again
Command-Option-Shift-R	Reset program change numbers

Actions

Keyboard Shortcut	Action
Control-P	Panic
Control-T	Tap Tempo
Control-M	Master Mute
Control-R	Toggle Recording
Space Bar	Toggle Play/Stop

Parameter Mapping

Keyboard Shortcut	Action
Command-L	Map the selected parameter
Command-F	Find in parameter mapping browser
Command-G	Find again
Command-Option-Left Bracket	Set the minimum value of the parameter range
Command-Option-Right Bracket	Set the maximum value of the parameter range

Channel Strips

Keyboard Shortcut	Action
Command-Option-A	Add audio channel strip
Command-Option-I	Add software instrument channel strip
Command-Option-F	Show or hide signal flow channel
Left Arrow	Select the channel strip to the left of the currently selected one
Right Arrow	Select the channel strip to the right of the currently selected one

Screen Controls

Keyboard Shortcut	Action
Command-L	Learn controller assignment (turn on the Learn process)
Command-Option-G	Group screen controls
Command-Option-Shift-G	Ungroup screen controls
Command-Option-H	Select the next screen control, select the Add hardware label checkbox, and select the Add hardware label text field for entering text
Option-Click	Reset screen control to its saved value

Perform in Full Screen

Keyboard Shortcut	Action
Up Arrow	Select the previous patch
Down Arrow	Select the next patch
Left Arrow	Select the first patch of the previous set
Right Arrow	Select the first patch of the next set
P	Send MIDI panic
M	Mute/unmute all audio
Escape	Exit Perform in Full Screen

Window and View

Keyboard Shortcut	Action
Command-1	Layout mode
Command-2	Edit mode
Command-3	Perform in Window
Command-4	Perform in Full Screen
Command-5	Show or hide Inspectors
Command-6	Show or hide the Channel Strips area
Command-7	Show or hide the workspace
Command-T	Show or hide the Tuner

Keyboard Shortcut	Action
Command-M	Minimize the frontmost window to the Dock
Command-Comma	Open the preferences window
V	Show or hide the active plug-in window
Command-Shift-M	Show the MIDI Message Monitor window

Help

Keyboard Shortcut	Action
Command-Shift-H	Shows or hides Quick Help
Command-Backslash	View detailed Help for a Quick Help topic

Motion

| Version 5.4.5

General Keyboard Shortcuts

Keyboard Shortcut	Action
Command-O	Open a project
Command-N	Create a project
Command-Option-N	Create a project from the Project Browser
Command-J	Open the project's Properties Inspector
Command-S	Save a project
Command-Shift-S	Save a project as a new project
Command-W	Close the frontmost window
Command-I	Import a file
Command-Shift-I	Import a file as a project
Command-E	Export movie
Command-Option-E	Export a selection as a movie
Command-Z	Undo the previous command
Command-Shift-Z	Redo, revoking the undo command
Command-X	Cut the selection
Command-C	Copy the selection
Command-V	Paste the selection
Command-D	Duplicate selection
Command-A	Select all items
Command-Shift-A	Deselect all items
Delete	Delete the selection

Keyboard Shortcut	Action
Command-M	Minimize the frontmost window to the Dock
Command-Comma	Open the preferences window
Command-Shift-P	Display Page Setup dialog
Command-H	Hide this app
Command-Option-H	Hide all other apps
Command-Q	Quit this app
Space Bar	Play/pause a project
A	Turn on or off animation recording
Home	Go to the start of a project
End	Go to the end of a project
Command-Option-T	Show or hide the toolbar

Motion Menu

Keyboard Shortcut	Action
Command-Comma	Open the preferences window
Command-H	Hide this app
Command-Option-H	Hide all other apps
Command-Q	Quit this app

File Menu

Keyboard Shortcut	Action
Command-N	Create a project from the Project Browser
Command-O	Open a project
Command-W	Close the frontmost window
Command-S	Save a project
Command-Shift-S	Save a project as a new project
Command-I	Import a file
Command-Shift-I	Import files as a project

Keyboard Shortcut	Action
Command-Option-W	Close all open projects
Command-Shift-P	Open the Page Setup window
Command-P	Print the current canvas view

Edit Menu

Keyboard Shortcut	Action
Command-Z	Undo the previous command
Command-Shift-Z	Redo, revoking the undo command
Command-X	Cut the selected text or item and copy it to the clipboard
Command-C	Copy the selected text or item to the clipboard
Command-V	Paste the contents of the clipboard
Command-Option-V	Paste special
Command-D	Duplicate the selected item
Delete	Delete
Shift-Delete	Ripple delete (remove the current selection and close the gap in the Timeline)
Command-Option-Shift-T	Transform control points (on a complex shape)
Command-A	Select all items
Command-Shift-A	Deselect all items
Command-J	Open the project's Properties Inspector
Command-Colon	Show spelling and grammar
Command-F	Find and replace
Press Function Twice	Start voice dictation
Command-Control-Space Bar	Show the Character Viewer, which you can choose emoji and other symbols

Mark Menu

Keyboard Shortcut	Action
I	Mark In point of a selected object or set the play range when no object is selected
O	Mark Out point of a selected object or set the play range when no object is selected
Shift-Left Bracket	Move the selected object's In point to the location of the playhead
Shift-Right Bracket	Move the selected object's Out point to the location of the playhead
M	Add a project marker at the current frame (with no selection) or add object marker (with selection)
Grave Accent	Add a project marker at the current frame (with no selection) or add object marker (with selection)
Command-Option-M	Open the Edit Marker dialog
Command-Option-I	Mark In point of play range
Command-Option-O	Mark Out point of play range
Option-X	Reset play range
Backslash	Play selection
Shift-L	Turn on Loop Playback
A	Turn animation recording on and off
Option-A	Open the Recording Options window
Function-Left Arrow	Go to the start of a project
Function-Right Arrow	Go to the end of a project
Shift-Function-Left Arrow	Go to the start of the play range
Shift-Function-Right Arrow	Go to the end of the play range
Left Arrow	Go to the previous frame
Right Arrow	Go to the next frame
Shift-Left Arrow	Go backward ten frames
Shift-Right Arrow	Go forward ten frames
Option-K	Go to the previous keyframe
Shift-K	Go to the next keyframe
Command-Option-Left Arrow	Go to the previous marker
Command-Option-Right Arrow	Go to the next marker
Shift-I	Go to the selection In point

Keyboard Shortcut	Action
Shift-O	Go to the selection Out point
Command-R	Perform a RAM preview of the play range area
Command-Option-R	Perform a RAM preview of the current selection
Command-Option-Shift-R	Perform a RAM preview for the whole project

Object Menu

Keyboard Shortcut	Action
Command-Shift-N	Add an empty group to the project
Command-Option-C	Add a camera to the project
Command-Shift-L	Add a light to the project
Command-Shift-D	Add a drop zone to the project
Command-Control-R	Add a rig to the project
Command-Shift-E	Add a 360° environment to the project
Command-Shift-Right Bracket	Move the selected object to the top of the Layers list
Command-Shift-Left Bracket	Move the selected object to the bottom of the Layers list
Command-Right Bracket	Move the selected object up the Layers list by one level
Command-Left Bracket	Move the selected object down the Layers list by one level
Command-Shift-G	Group the selected objects into a new layer
Command-Option-G	Ungroup a group of objects
Control-T	Make an object active or deactivate an object
Control-S	For an audio track, enable/disable the Solo button of the selected track; for an object, solo the object
Control-I	Isolate the selected group or layer
Control-L	Lock/unlock an object
Control-Shift-S	Unsolo only the video portion of a file that contains video
Control-D	Convert a 2D group to 3D, or convert a 3D group to 2D
Command-Shift-M	Add an image mask to the selected object
Control-K	Add a keyframe (to the last modified parameter for the selected object)
Command-K	Convert the applied behaviors to keyframes
Command-Option-B	Convert a simple shape to a complex shape (with editable control points)

Keyboard Shortcut	Action
E	Make the selected object the cell source for a particle emitter
L	Replicate the selected object
K	Clone the selected layer
Shift-F	Open the Media list and Inspector to display the source and properties of media objects

View Menu

Keyboard Shortcut	Action
Command-Equal Sign	Zoom in
Command-Minus Sign	Zoom out
Option-Z	Zoom to 100 percent
Shift-Z	Zoom to fit in window
Command-Option-Equal Sign	Zoom Timeline in
Command-Option-Minus Sign	Zoom Timeline out
Command-Option-0	Zoom Timeline to project duration
Shift-V	Show full view area (the portion of layers that extend beyond the edge of the canvas)
Control-A	Set 3D view to active camera
Control-P	Set 3D view to perspective camera
Control-V	Set 3D view to 360° Look Around
Control-O	Set 3D view to 360° Overview
Control-H	Set 3D view to Mirror VR Headset
Control-C	Set 3D view to next camera
Option-Control-C	Select the current active camera
Control-R	Reset 3D camera view
F	Fit the selected objects into view
Command-Shift-F	Frame the selected object
Control-F	Focus on the selected object
Shift-C	Show all color channels
Shift-T	Show the transparent channel
Option-Shift-T	Show the alpha channel overlay

Keyboard Shortcut	Action
Option-Shift-C	Show the RGB channels only
Shift-R	Show the red channel
Shift-G	Show the green channel
Shift-B	Show the blue channel
Shift-A	Show the alpha channel
Option-Shift-A	Show the inverted alpha channel
V	Switch between the current channel and alpha channels
Option-Shift-O	Show the out of gamut exposure overlay in the canvas
Shift-Q	Show the canvas at full resolution
Option-L	Enable/disable lighting in the canvas
Option-Control-S	Enable/disable shadows in the canvas
Option-Control-R	Enable/disable reflections in the canvas
Option-Control-D	Enable/disable depth of field in the canvas
Option-M	Enable/disable motion blur in the canvas
Option-F	Enable/disable field rendering in the canvas
Option-Control-B	Enable/disable frame blending in the canvas
Command-Forward Slash	Show overlays
Command-Shift-R	Show the rulers
Command-Apostrophe	Show or hide the grid
Command-Semicolon	Show or hide the guides
Command-Shift-Semicolon	Show or hide the dynamic guides
Apostrophe	Show or hide the safe zones
Shift-Quotation Mark	Show or hide the film zones
Command-Option-Semicolon	Lock the guides
N	Enable/disable snapping to guides
Command-Option-Forward Slash	Show 3D overlays
Command-Shift-Apostrophe	Show 3D grid
Command-T	Show the Font dialog
Command-Shift-C	Show the macOS Colors window

Share Menu

Keyboard Shortcut	Action
Command-E	Export movie

Window Menu

Keyboard Shortcut	Action
Command-M	Minimize the frontmost window to the Dock
Control-U	Set the Motion window to Classic layout
Option-Control-U	Set Motion window to Cinema layout
F1	Show the Properties Inspector
F2	Show the Behaviors Inspector
F3	Show the Filters Inspector
F4	Show the Object Inspector
F5	Show or hide the Project pane
F6	Show or hide the Timing pane
F7	Show or hide the HUD
F9	Show or hide the Background Task list
F8	Enter/exit Player mode
F10	Output to VR headset
Command-2	Show or hide the Library
Command-3	Show or hide the Inspector
Command-4	Show or hide the Layers list or Project pane
Command-5	Show or hide the Media list
Command-6	Show or hide the Audio list
Command-7	Show or hide the Video Timeline
Command-8	Show or hide the Keyframe Editor
Command-9	Show or hide the Audio Timeline
Command-Control-F	Enter/exit full screen

Help Menu

Keyboard Shortcut	Action
Command-Shift-Question Mark	Open Motion Help

Audio List

Keyboard Shortcut	Action
Command-6	Show or hide the Audio list
Control-T	Make object active or inactive
Control-L	Lock/unlock an audio file
Control-S	Enable/disable the Solo button of a selected track
Up Arrow	Move selection up one level in the Audio list
Down Arrow	Move selection down one level in the Audio list
Command-I	Import

Transform Tool

Keyboard Shortcut	Action
S	Activate the current transform tool (when another item in the transform tools pop-up menu is selected)
Shift-S	Choose the Select/Transform tool
Tab	Cycle through the transform modes (press repeatedly until the transform mode you want is selected)
Shift-Drag the object	Constrain the movement of an object to the X axis or Y axis
Command-Drag the object	Override snapping while moving an object
Option-Drag the object	Duplicate a selected object

Select/Transform Tool

Keyboard Shortcut	Action
Shift-Drag the object handle	Scale an object proportionally
Option-Drag the object handle	Scale an object from its anchor point

Keyboard Shortcut	Action
Option-Shift-Drag the object handle	Scale an object proportionally from its anchor point
Shift-Drag the object rotation handle	Snap the rotation of an object to 45-degree increments
Q	Select the 3D transform tool

Crop Tool

Keyboard Shortcut	Action
Shift-Drag the object handle	Crop an object proportionally
Option-Drag the object handle	Crop an object from its center
Option-Shift-Drag the object handle	Crop an object proportionally from its center
Command-Drag over the object	Pan a cropped object within the bounding box
Command-Option-Drag over the object	Move the bounding with the cropped object

Edit Points Tool

Keyboard Shortcut	Action
Option-Click the path	Add a point to a path
Command-Click the point	Convert a point to linear
Command-Drag the point	Convert a linear point to Bézier
Command-Drag the tangent handle	Scale a tangent proportionally
Option-Drag the tangent handle	Break or relink a tangent handle
Shift-Drag the tangent handle	Constrain a tangent handle to 45-degree increments
Command-Drag the B-Spline point	Adjust a B-Spline point bias
Command-Click the B-Spline point	Switch a B-Spline point bias

Edit Shape Tool

Keyboard Shortcut	Action
Command-Option-B	Convert a simple ellipse, rectangle, or mask to a complex shape or mask (with editable control points)

Pan and Zoom Tool

Keyboard Shortcut	Action
H	Select the Pan tool
Z	Select the Zoom tool
Option-Click in the canvas	Zoom out with the Zoom tool selected

Shape Tool

Keyboard Shortcut	Action
R	Select the Rectangle Shape tool
C	Select the Circle Shape tool
Shift-Drag in the canvas	Draw a shape proportionally
Option-Drag in the canvas	Draw a shape from its center
Option-Shift-Drag in the canvas	Draw a shape proportionally from its center
Shift-Drag a rotation handle	Snap the rotation of an object to 45-degree increments

Bézier Tool

Keyboard Shortcut	Action
B	Select the Bézier tool
B	Switch between the Bézier and B-spline tools
C	Close shape
Command-Click a path	Add a point to the path
Command-Click a point	Convert a point to linear
Command-Drag a point	Create tangents on a point
Command-Drag a tangent handle	Scale a tangent handle proportionally
Option-Drag a tangent handle	Break or relink a tangent handle
Shift-Drag a tangent handle	Constrain a tangent handle to 45-degree increments
Escape	Cancel shape drawing and delete the open shape
Return	Exit shape-drawing mode

B-Spline Tool

Keyboard Shortcut	Action
B	Select the B-Spline tool
B	Switch between the Bézier and B-Spline tools
C	Close the shape
Command-Click a path	Add a point to the path
Command-Drag a B-Spline point	Adjust a B-Spline point bias
Command-Click a B-Spline point	Switch a B-Spline point bias
Escape	Cancel shape drawing and delete the open shape
Return	Exit shape-drawing mode

Paint Stroke Tool

Keyboard Shortcut	Action
P	Select the Paint Stroke tool
With the Adjust Item tool selected, Command-Drag in the canvas on a control point (+)	Adjust stroke width

Text Tool

Keyboard Shortcut	Action
T	Select the Text tool
Up Arrow, Down Arrow, Left Arrow, or Right Arrow	Move the insertion point to the next character
Option-Right Arrow	Move the insertion point to the next word
Option-Left Arrow	Move the insertion point to the previous word
Command-Left Arrow	Move to the beginning of a line of text
Command-Right Arrow	Move to the end of a line of text
Option-Up Arrow	Move to the beginning of a paragraph
Option-Down Arrow	Move to the end of a paragraph
Command-Up Arrow	Move to the beginning of a text object

Keyboard Shortcut	Action
Command-Down Arrow	Move to the end of a text object
Shift-Right Arrow Left Arrow	Select characters from the insertion point
Option-Shift-Left Arrow Right Arrow	Select words from the insertion point
Command-Shift-Left Arrow	Select text from the insertion point to the beginning of a line
Command-Shift-Right Arrow	Select text from the insertion point to the end of a line
Option-Shift-Up Arrow Down Arrow	When Layout Method is set to Paragraph (in the Text Inspector's Layout Controls), select the rest of a paragraph from the insertion point
Command-Shift-Up Arrow Down Arrow	Select the rest of a text object from the insertion point
Command-Option-Right Bracket	Increase kerning from the insertion point
Command-Option-Left Bracket	Decrease kerning from the insertion point
Command-A	Select all items
Command-Shift-A	Deselect All
Escape	Exit the Text tool

Shape Mask Tool

Keyboard Shortcut	Action
Option-R	Select the Rectangle Mask tool
Option-C	Select the Circle Mask tool
Option-P	Select the Freehand Mask tool
Shift-Drag in the canvas	Draw a mask proportionally
Option-Drag in the canvas	Draw a mask from its center
Option-Shift-Drag in the canvas	Draw a mask proportionally from its center
Shift-Drag a rotation handle	Snap the rotation of a mask to 45-degree increments

Bézier Mask Tool

Keyboard Shortcut	Action
Option-B	Select the Bézier Mask tool
Option-B	Switch between the Bézier Mask and B-Spline Mask tools
C	Close the mask shape
Command-Click a path	Add a point to the path
Command-Click a point	Convert a point to linear
Command-Drag a point	Create tangents on a point
Command-Drag a tangent handle	Scale tangents proportionally
Option-Drag a tangent handle	Break or relink a tangent handle
Option-Shift-Drag a tangent handle	Constrain a tangent handle to 45-degree increments
Escape	Cancel shape drawing and delete the open mask
Return	Exit mask-drawing mode

B-Spline Mask Tool

Keyboard Shortcut	Action
Option-B	Switch between the Bézier Mask and B-Spline Mask tools
C	Close the mask shape
Command-Click a path	Add a point to the path
Command-Drag a B-Spline point	Adjust a B-Spline point bias
Command-Click a B-Spline point	Switch a B-Spline point bias
Escape	Cancel mask drawing and delete the open shape
Return	Exit mask-drawing mode

Transport Control

Keyboard Shortcut	Action
Space Bar	Play/pause a project
A	Turn animation recording on or off
Shift-L	Enable/disable loop playback

Keyboard Shortcut	Action
Home	Go to the start of a project
End	Go to the end of a project
Shift-Home	Go to the start of the play range
Shift-End	Go to the end of the play range
Left Arrow	Go to the previous frame
Right Arrow	Go to the next frame
Shift-Left Arrow	Go backward ten frames
Shift-Right Arrow	Go forward ten frames

View Option

Keyboard Shortcut	Action
Command-Equal Sign	Zoom in
Command-Minus Sign	Zoom out
Option-Click the canvas	Zoom out with the Zoom tool selected
Command-Drag in the canvas with the Zoom tool	Zoom to region
Option-Z	Zoom to 100 percent
Shift-Z	Zoom to fit in the canvas
Shift-C	Show all color channels
Shift-T	Show the transparent channel
Option-Shift-T	Show the alpha channel overlay
Option-Shift-C	Show the RGB channels only
Shift-R	Show the red channel
Shift-G	Show the green channel
Shift-B	Show the blue channel
Shift-A	Show the alpha channel
Option-Shift-A	Show the inverted alpha channel
V	Switch between the current channel and alpha channel
Shift-Q	Show the canvas at full resolution
Option-F	Enable/disable field rendering in the canvas

Keyboard Shortcut	Action
Option-M	Enable/disable motion blur in the canvas
Command-Shift-R	Show the rulers
Command-Option-Semicolon	Lock the guides
Command-Apostrophe	Show or hide the grid
Command-Semicolon	Show or hide the guides
Command-Shift-Semicolon	Show or hide dynamic guides
Shift-Quotation Mark	Show or hide film zones
Command-Forward Slash	Show overlays
Apostrophe	Show or hide safe zones
N	Enable/disable snapping to guides
X	Expose active layers
Shift-X	Expose all layers

HUD

Keyboard Shortcut	Action
F7	Show or hide the HUD
D	Cycle through the HUDs from top to bottom (when more than one effect is applied to an object)
Shift-D	Cycle through the HUDs from bottom to top (when more than one effect is applied to an object)

Inspector

Keyboard Shortcut	Action
Command-3	Show or hide the Inspector
Up Arrow	Increase a slider value by an increment of one
Down Arrow	Decrease a slider value by an increment of one
Shift-Up Arrow	Increase a slider value by an increment of ten
Shift-Down Arrow	Decrease a slider value by an increment of ten

Keyframe Editor

Keyboard Shortcut	Action
Command-8	Show or hide the Keyframe Editor
Command-K	Convert the applied behaviors to keyframes
F	Fit visible curves

Layers

Keyboard Shortcut	Action
Command-Shift-N	Create a group
Command-Right Bracket	Bring an object up one level in the Layers list
Command-Left Bracket	Send an object down one level in the Layers list
Command-Shift-G	Place the selected objects in a new group
Command-Option-G	Ungroup a group of objects so you can manipulate each object
Control-T	Make the object active or deactivate the object
Control-S	Enable/disable the Solo button of a selected track
Control-I	Isolate the selected group or layer
Control-L	Lock/unlock an object
Up Arrow	Move up one level in the Layers list
Down Arrow	Move down one level in the Layers list
Option-Left Arrow	Expand a group in the Layers list
Option-Right Arrow	Collapse a group in the Layers list
Command-I	Import
Command-Shift-M	Add an image mask to the selected object
Command-K	Convert the applied behaviors to keyframes
Shift-F	Open the Media list and Inspector to reveal the source and properties of media objects
K	Clone the selected layer

Library

Keyboard Shortcut	Action
Command-2	Show or hide the Library
Space Bar	Select the first item in the sidebar or file stack
Up Arrow	Move up one item in the sidebar or file stack
Down Arrow	Move down one item in the sidebar or file stack
Left Arrow	Move left one item in the file stack
Right Arrow	Move right one item in the file stack
Up Arrow	Move up one level in the folder hierarchy of the file stack

Media List

Keyboard Shortcut	Action
Command-5	Show or hide the Media list
Up Arrow	Move up one level in the Media list
Down Arrow	Move down one level in the Media list
Command-I	Import

Timeline

Keyboard Shortcut	Action
Command-Right Arrow	Nudge one frame forward
Command-Left Arrow	Nudge one frame backward
Command-Shift-Right Arrow	Nudge ten frames forward
Command-Shift-Left Arrow	Nudge ten frames backward
Shift-Left Bracket	Move the selected object to the In point
Shift-Right Bracket	Move the selected object to the Out point
I	Mark the In point of the play range or selected object
O	Mark the Out point of the play range or selected object
Option-X	Reset the play range by moving the In and Out points to the first and last frames of the project

Keyboard Shortcut	Action
Command-Right Bracket	Bring an object up one level in the Timeline layers list
Command-Left Bracket	Send an object down one level in the Timeline layers list
Shift-L	Enable/disable loop playback
Option-A	Open the Recording Options dialog
Shift-Home	Go to the start of the play range
Shift-End	Go to the end of the play range
Shift-I	Go to the In point of the selected object
Shift-O	Go to the Out point of the selected object
Left Arrow	Go to the previous frame
Right Arrow	Go to the next frame
Shift-Left Arrow	Go backward ten frames
Shift-Right Arrow	Go forward ten frames
Command-Option-Left Arrow	Go to the next marker
Command-Option-Right Arrow	Go to the previous marker
Command-R	Render a RAM preview for the play range
Command-Option-R	Render a RAM preview for the selected object
Command-Option-Shift-R	Render a RAM preview for the project
M	Add a marker at the current frame
Apostrophe	Add a marker at the current frame
Command-Option-M	Open the Edit Marker dialog
Space Bar	Play/pause the project
A	Turn on or off animation recording
Home	Go to the start of project
End	Go to the end of project
Command-K	Convert the applied behaviors to keyframes
Shift-Delete	Ripple delete (remove the current selection and close the gap in the Timeline)
Option-Shift-V	Paste special
Command-Option-Equal Sign	Zoom Timeline in
Command-Option-Minus Sign	Zoom Timeline out
Shift-Z	Fit Timeline in window
Command-Option-0	Zoom Timeline to project duration

Keyframing

Keyboard Shortcut	Action
Option-Click a path	Add a point to the path
Command-Drag a Bézier point	Create tangents on a point
Command-Click a Bézier point	Convert a point to linear
Command-Drag a B-Spline point	Adjust a B-Spline point bias
Command-Click a B-Spline point	Switch a B-Spline point bias
Command-Drag a tangent handle	Scale tangents proportionally
Option-Drag a tangent handle	Break or relink a tangent handle
Shift-Drag a tangent handle	Constrain a tangent to 45 degrees and original value

Shape and Mask

Keyboard Shortcut	Action
Shift-Drag in the canvas	Draw a shape proportionally with the Rectangle, Circle Shape, and Mask tools
Option-Drag in the canvas	Draw a shape from its center with the Rectangle, Circle Shape, and Mask tools
Option-Shift-Drag in the canvas	Draw a shape proportionally from its center with the Rectangle, Circle Shape, and Mask tools
Escape	Cancel spline drawing and delete the open spline
Return	Exit spline drawing mode and complete the existing spline drawing
Option-Click a path	Add a point to the path
Command-Click a Bézier point	Convert a point to linear
Command-Drag a Bézier point	Create tangents on a point
Command-Drag a tangent handle	Scale tangents proportionally
Command-Drag a B-Spline point	Adjust a B-Spline point bias
Command-Click a B-Spline point	Switch a B-Spline point bias
Option-Drag a tangent handle	Break or relink a tangent handle
Shift-Drag a tangent handle	Constrain a tangent to 45 degrees and original value
Command-Option-B	Convert a simple shape to a complex shape (with editable control points)

3D

Keyboard Shortcut	Action
Q	Select the 3D transform tool
Comma	Switch the 3D transform tool between position-only and universal
Period	Switch the 3D transform tool between rotate-only and universal
Forward Slash	Switch the 3D transform tool between scale-only and universal
Control-A	Set 3D View to Active Camera
Control-P	Set 3D View to Perspective
Control-C	Set 3D View to next camera
Control-R	Reset the 3D camera view
Control-D	Switches a group between 2D and 3D
Command-Shift-Apostrophe	Switch the 3D grid on and off

Miscellaneous

Keyboard Shortcut	Action
E	Create a particle emitter
Command-Shift-M	Add an image mask to the selected layer
Z and click the color wheel	In the Keyer filter, zoom incrementally into the Chroma control
Option-Z and click the color wheel	In the Keyer filter, zoom incrementally out of the Chroma control
Z and drag right in the color wheel	In the Keyer filter, zoom smoothly into the Chroma control
Z and drag left in the color wheel	In the Keyer filter, zoom smoothly out of the Chroma control
Space Bar-Command and drag right/left	In the Keyer filter, zoom smoothly in or out of the Chroma control
H and drag the color wheel	In the Keyer filter, pan the Chroma control
Shift-Z	In the Keyer filter, reset the chroma zoom and center
Up Arrow	Select the next object above
Down Arrow	Select the next object below
Command-Arrow Keys	Nudge the selected objects one pixel
Command-Shift-Arrow Keys	Nudge the selected objects 10 pixels
Shift-Drag in the canvas	Add/Remove selected objects using the region box
Command-Click an object or objects	Select multiple objects in a group or layer
Shift-Click an object	Add to selection

Remote Desktop

| Version 3.9.3

General Keyboard Shortcuts

Keyboard Shortcut	Action
Command-N	New List
Command-Shift-N	New List from Selection
Command-Option-N	New Scanner
Command-Control-N	New Smart List
Command-Option-Control-N	New Group
Command-D	Duplicate the selected item
Command-Y	Refresh
Command-Option-Shift-N	Add by Address
Command-I	Get Info
Command-W	Close the frontmost window
Command-S	Save the task
Command-Shift-S	Save Task As
Command-Option-E	Export Window
Command-Shift-P	Show page setup for printing
Command-P	Print the document
Command-Option-T	Show Toolbar
Command-J	View Options
Command-Option-I	System Overview
Command-Option-F	File Search
Command-L	Lock Screen

Keyboard Shortcut	Action
Command-U	Unlock Screen
Command-F	Spotlight Search
Command-R	Run
Command-Option-R	Retry Failed
Command-Option-Shift-R	Retry All
Command-Shift-D	Duplicate Task
Command-Option-Period	Stop Task
Command-1	Remote Desktop
Command-2	Messages From Users
Command-3	Active Share Screen Tasks
Command-4	Task History
Command-Option-L	File Transfers

Swift Playgrounds

| Version 3.3

Keyboard Shortcut	Action
Command-N	New Blank Playground
Command-Arrow Down	Open Selected Playground
Command-Shift-I	Import Playground
Command-Control-N	New Module
Command-Option-Control-N	New Source File
Command-I	Add Source File
Command-Shift-N	New Page
Command-Delete	Delete Playground
Command-D	Duplicate Playground
Control-I	Re-Indent
Command-Left Bracket	Shift Left
Command-Right Bracket	Shift Right
Command-/	Block Comment
Command-Option-Control-R	Run Fastest
Command-Control-R	Run Faster
Command-R	Run My Code
Command-Shift-R	Step Through My Code
Command-Option-Shift-R	Step Slowly
Command-Period	Stop
Command-Return	Show Live View
Command-Escape	Show Expanded Code Completions
Command-Option-Arrow Right	Show Next Page

Keyboard Shortcut	Action
Command-Option-Left Arrow	Show Previous Page
Command-Option-Right Arrow	Show Next Page
Command-Option-Left Arrow	Show Previous Page
Control-Tab	Show Next Tab
Control-Shift-Tab	Show Previous Tab
Command-Shift-O	Show Developer Documentation

Xcode

Version 11.5

Keyboard Shortcut	Action
Command-Comma	Open the preferences window
Command-H	Hide this app
Command-Option-H	Hide all other apps
Command-Q	Quit this app
Command-Control-T	New Editor
Command-Option-Control-T	New Editor Below
Command-T	New Tab
Command-Shift-T	New Window
Command-N	New File
Command-Option-Shift-N	New Playground
Command-Shift-N	New Project
Command-Control-Shift-N	Swift Package
Command-Control-N	New Workspace
Command-Option-N	New Group
Command-Option-A	Add Files
Command-O	Open...
Command-Shift-O	Open Quickly...
Command-W	Close the frontmost window
Command-Option-W	Close Other Tabs
Command-Option-Control-Shift-W	Close Other Editors
Command-Control-W	Close Document
Command-Control-Shift-W	Close Workspace

Keyboard Shortcut	Action
Command-S	Save the document
Command-Shift-S	Duplicate the document
Command-Shift-P	Show page setup for printing
Command-P	Print the document
Command-Z	Undo the previous command
Command-Shift-Z	Redo, revoking the undo command
Command-X	Cut the selected text or item and copy it to the clipboard
Command-C	Copy the selected text or item to the clipboard
Command-V	Paste the contents of the clipboard
Command-Option-V	Paste Special
Command-Option-Shift-V	Paste and preserve formatting
Command-D	Duplicate the selected item
Command-Delete	Delete
Command-A	Select all items
Command-Control-Shift-T	Show fonts
Command-Control-Shift-Return	Focus
Control-1	Show Related Items
Command-Control-2	Show Previous Files History
Command-Control-3	Show Next Files History
Control-4	Show Top Level Items
Control-5	Show Group Files
Control-6	Show Document Items
Command-Option-Shift-Z	Reset Assistant Selection
Command-1	Show Project Navigator
Command-2	Show Source Control Navigator
Command-3	Show symbol navigator
Command-4	Show find navigator
Command-5	Show issue navigator
Command-6	Show Test Navigator
Command-7	Show Debug Navigator
Command-8	Show Breakpoint Navigator

Keyboard Shortcut	Action
Command-9	Show Report Navigator
Command-0	Show navigator
Command-Option-J	Filter in navigator
Command-Shift-C	Activate console
Command-Shift-Y	Show debug area
Command-Option-O	Show Inspectors
Command-Shift-L	Show Library
Command-Option-T	Show Toolbar
Command-Shift-Backslash	Show All Tabs
Command-Shift-J	Reveal in Project Navigator
Command-Shift-D	Reveal in Debug Navigator
Command-Option-Comma	Open in Next Editor
Command-Option-Shift-Grave Accent	Move Focus To Previous Area
Control-Shift-Grave Accent	Move Focus To Previous Editor
Command-J	Move Focus to Editor
Command-Option-Control-Right Arrow	Go Forward in Alternate Editor
Command-Control-Right Arrow	Go Forward
Command-Control-Left Arrow	Go Back
Command-Option-L	Jump to Selection
Command-Control-J	Jump to Definition
Command-Apostrophe	Jump to Next Issue
Command-Shift-Apostrophe	Jump to Previous Issue
Command-Control-P	Jump to Instruction Pointer
Command-Control-Up Arrow	Jump to Next Counterpart
Command-Control-Down Arrow	Jump to Previous Counterpart
Command-L	Jump to
Command-/	Jump to Next Placeholder
Command-Shift-/	Jump to Previous Placeholder
Control-Backslash	Jump to Next Change
Control-Shift-Backslash	Jump to Previous Change
Command-Return	Show Editor Only

Keyboard Shortcut	Action
Command-Option-Return	Preview
Command-Option-Control-Return	Assistant
Command-R	Run
Command-U	Test
Command-I	Profile
Command-Shift-B	Analyze
Command-Shift-R	Build for Running
Command-Shift-U	Build for Testing
Command-Shift-I	Build for Profiling
Command-Control-R	Run without Building
Command-Control-I	Test without Building
Command-Control-I	Profile without Building
Command-Control-B	Compile File
Command-Control-Shift-B	Analyze File
Command-B	Build
Command-Shift-K	Clean Build Folder
Command-Period	Stop
Control-O	Choose Scheme
Command-Control-Right Bracket	Select Next Scheme
Command-Control-Left Bracket	Select Previous Scheme
Command-Shift-Comma	Edit Scheme
Control-Shift-0	Choose Destination
Command-Option-Control-Right Bracket	Select Next Destination
Command-Option-Control-Left Bracket	Select Previous Destination
Command-Shift-Period	Edit Test Plan
Command-Control-Y	Pause
Command-Control-C	Continue to Current Line
F6	Step Over
F7	Step Into
F8	Step Out
Control-F6	Step Over Instruction

Keyboard Shortcut	Action
Control-Shift-F6	Step Over Thread
Control-F7	Step Into Instruction
Control-Shift-F7	Step Into Thread
Command-Y	Deactivate Breakpoints
Command-Backslash	Add Breakpoint at Current Line
Command-Option-Backslash	Create Symbolic Breakpoint
Command-Option-Control-Shift-M	View Memory
Command-K	Clear Console
Command-Option-K	Reload Console
Command-Option-C	Commit
Command-Option-X	Pull
Command-M	Minimize the frontmost window to the Dock
Command-Option-Shift-T	Rename-Tab
Control-Shift-Tab	Show Previous Tab
Control-Tab	Show Next Tab
Command-Shift-0	Developer Documentation
Command-Shift-1	Welcome to Xcode
Command-Shift-2	Devices and Simulators
Command-Option-Shift-O	Organizer
Command-Shift-8	Show TouchBar
Command-Control-Shift-Forward Slash	Show Quick Help for Selected Item
Command-Option-Control-Forward Slash	Search Documentation for Selected Text

Accessibility Inspector

| Version 5.0

Keyboard Shortcut	Action
Command-Comma	Open the preferences window
Command-H	Hide this app
Command-Option-H	Hide all other apps
Command-Q	Quit this app
Command-N	New
Command-O	Open
Command-W	Close the frontmost window
Command-Shift-S	Save Audit Report As
Command-Shift-P	Show page setup for printing
Command-P	Print the document
Command-Z	Undo the previous command
Command-Shift-Z	Redo, revoking the undo command
Command-X	Cut the selected text or item and copy it to the clipboard
Command-C	Copy the selected text or item to the clipboard
Command-V	Paste the contents of the clipboard
Command-Option-Shift-P	Paste and Match Style
Command-A	Select all items
Command-F	Find items in a document or app
Command-Option-F	Find and Replace
Command-G	Find again: find the next occurrence of the item already found
Command-Shift-G	Find the previous occurrence
Command-E	Use selection for find

Keyboard Shortcut	Action
Command-Comma	Open the preferences window
Command-H	Hide this app
Command-Option-H	Hide all other apps
Command-Q	Quit this app
Command-N	New
Command-O	Open
Command-W	Close the frontmost window
Command-Shift-S	Save Audit Report As
Command-Shift-P	Show page setup for printing
Command-P	Print the document
Command-Z	Undo the previous command
Command-Shift-Z	Redo, revoking the undo command
Command-X	Cut the selected text or item and copy it to the clipboard
Command-C	Copy the selected text or item to the clipboard
Command-V	Paste the contents of the clipboard
Command-Option-Shift-P	Paste and Match Style
Command-A	Select all items
Command-F	Find items in a document or app
Command-Option-F	Find and Replace
Command-G	Find again: find the next occurrence of the item already found
Command-Shift-G	Find the previous occurrence
Command-E	Use selection for find
Command-J	Jump to Selection
Command-Colon	Show spelling and grammar
Command-Shift-Colon	Check document now
Press Function Twice	Start voice dictation
Command-Control-Space Bar	Show the Character Viewer, which you can choose emoji and other symbols
Command-Option-Control-Shift-P	Enable Point to Inspect
Command-Control-Arrow Right	Move to Next Item
Command-Control-Arrow Left	Move to Previous Item
Command-Control-Arrow Right	Move to Parent Item

Accessibility Inspector

Version 5.0

Keyboard Shortcut	Action
Command-Comma	Open the preferences window
Command-H	Hide this app
Command-Option-H	Hide all other apps
Command-Q	Quit this app
Command-N	New
Command-O	Open
Command-W	Close the frontmost window
Command-Shift-S	Save Audit Report As
Command-Shift-P	Show page setup for printing
Command-P	Print the document
Command-Z	Undo the previous command
Command-Shift-Z	Redo, revoking the undo command
Command-X	Cut the selected text or item and copy it to the clipboard
Command-C	Copy the selected text or item to the clipboard
Command-V	Paste the contents of the clipboard
Command-Option-Shift-P	Paste and Match Style
Command-A	Select all items
Command-F	Find items in a document or app
Command-Option-F	Find and Replace
Command-G	Find again: find the next occurrence of the item already found
Command-Shift-G	Find the previous occurrence
Command-E	Use selection for find

Keyboard Shortcut	Action
Command-Comma	Open the preferences window
Command-H	Hide this app
Command-Option-H	Hide all other apps
Command-Q	Quit this app
Command-N	New
Command-O	Open
Command-W	Close the frontmost window
Command-Shift-S	Save Audit Report As
Command-Shift-P	Show page setup for printing
Command-P	Print the document
Command-Z	Undo the previous command
Command-Shift-Z	Redo, revoking the undo command
Command-X	Cut the selected text or item and copy it to the clipboard
Command-C	Copy the selected text or item to the clipboard
Command-V	Paste the contents of the clipboard
Command-Option-Shift-P	Paste and Match Style
Command-A	Select all items
Command-F	Find items in a document or app
Command-Option-F	Find and Replace
Command-G	Find again: find the next occurrence of the item already found
Command-Shift-G	Find the previous occurrence
Command-E	Use selection for find
Command-J	Jump to Selection
Command-Colon	Show spelling and grammar
Command-Shift-Colon	Check document now
Press Function Twice	Start voice dictation
Command-Control-Space Bar	Show the Character Viewer, which you can choose emoji and other symbols
Command-Option-Control-Shift-P	Enable Point to Inspect
Command-Control-Arrow Right	Move to Next Item
Command-Control-Arrow Left	Move to Previous Item
Command-Control-Arrow Right	Move to Parent Item

Keyboard Shortcut	Action
Command-Control-Arrow Down	Move to Child Item
Command-Refresh	Refresh
Command-Shift-R	Run Audit
Command-Shift-C	Clear All Audit Warnings
Command-Plus	Increase Font Size
Command-Minus	Decrease Font Size
Command-Option-T	Hide Toolbar
Command-M	Minimize
Command-1	Show Main Window
Command-Option-N	Show Notifications
Command-Option-C	Show Color Contrast Calculator

Create ML

Version 1.0

Keyboard Shortcut	Action
Command-H	Hide this app
Command-Option-H	Hide all other apps
Command-Q	Quit this app
Command-Shift-N	New Project
Command-N	New Model Source
Command-O	Open
Command-W	Close the frontmost window
Command-S	Save the document
Command-Option-Shift-S	Save the current document by specifying the name and location
Command-Z	Undo the previous command
Command-Shift-Z	Redo, revoking the undo command
Command-X	Cut the selected text or item and copy it to the clipboard
Command-C	Copy the selected text or item to the clipboard
Command-V	Paste the contents of the clipboard
Command-Option-Shift-V	Paste and Match Style
Command-A	Select all items
Command-F	Find items in a document or app
Command-Option-F	Find and replace
Command-G	Find again: find the next occurrence of the item already found
Command-Shift-G	Find the previous occurrence
Command-E	Use Selection for Find
Command-J	Jump to selection

Keyboard Shortcut	Action
Command-Colon	Show spelling and grammar
Command-Semicolon	Check Document Now
Press Function Twice	Start voice dictation
Command-Control-Space Bar	Show the Character Viewer, which you can choose emoji and other symbols
Command-Shift-Backslash	Show All Tabs
Command-Option-T	Hide Toolbar
Command-Control-S	Hide Sidebar
Command-Control-F	Enter full screen
Command-Option-L	Show Queue
Control-Shift-Tab	Show Previous Tab
Control-Tab	Show Next Tab
Command-M	Minimize the frontmost window to the Dock

FileMerge

Version 2.11

Keyboard Shortcut	Action
Command-Comma	Open the preferences window
Command-H	Hide this app
Command-Option-H	Hide all other apps
Command-Q	Quit this app
Command-O	Compare Files
Command-U	Recompare Files
Command-W	Close the frontmost window
Command-S	Save the merge
Command-Shift-S	Save Merge As
Command-Shift-P	Show page setup for printing
Command-P	Print the document
Command-Z	Undo the previous command
Command-Shift-Z	Redo, revoking the undo command
Command-X	Cut the selected text or item and copy it to the clipboard
Command-C	Copy the selected text or item to the clipboard
Command-V	Paste the contents of the clipboard
Command-A	Select all items
Command-Shift-C	Copy Selected changes
Press Function Twice	Start voice dictation
Command-Control-Space Bar	Show the Character Viewer, which you can choose emoji and other symbols
Command-Down Arrow	Find Next Difference
Command-D	Find Next Conflict

Keyboard Shortcut	Action
Command-Up Arrow	Find Previous Difference
Command-Shift-D	Find Previous Conflict
Command-L	Go to Line/Difference
Command-F	Find items in a document or app
Command-G	Find again: find the next occurrence of the item already found
Command-Shift-G	Find the previous occurrence
Command-E	Use selection for find
Command-J	Jump to Selection
Command-M	Minimize the frontmost window to the Dock
Command-Control-Z	Zoom
Control-Shift-Tab	Show Previous Tab
Control-Tab	Show Next Tab
Command-Shift-Backslash	Show All Tabs

Instruments

Version 11.5

Keyboard Shortcut	Action
Command-N	New
Command-O	Open
Command-W	Close the frontmost window
Command-S	Save the document
Command-Shift-S	Save the current document by specifying the name and location
Command-R	Record Trace
Command-Shift-R	Pause Trace
Command-Option-R	Recording Options
Command-Z	Undo the previous command
Command-Shift-Z	Redo, revoking the undo command
Command-X	Cut the selected text or item and copy it to the clipboard
Command-C	Copy the selected text or item to the clipboard
Command-Option-C	Copy with Header
Command-Shift-C	Deep Copy
Command-V	Paste the contents of the clipboard
Command-Option-Shift-V	Paste and Match Style
Command-A	Select all items
Command-F	Find items in a document or app
Command-G	Find again: find the next occurrence of the item already found
Command-Shift-G	Find the previous occurrence
Command-E	Use selection for find
Command-J	Jump to selection

Keyboard Shortcut	Action
Command-Shift-Semicolon	Show spelling and grammar
Command-Semicolon	Check spelling
Command-L	Show Library
Command-D	Show Detail Area
Command-Shift-Y	Show Pinned Area
Command-1	Show Extended Detail
Command-2	Show Run Info
Command-Control-Shift-Z	Zoom to fit
Command-Plus	Zoom in
Command-Minus	Zoom out
Space Bar	Pin selected track
Command-Shift-K	Clear Pinned Tracks
Command-Shift-Arrow Down	Clear Inspection Range
Command-I	Instrument Inspector
Command-Right Curly Bracket	Previous Run
Command-Left Curly Bracket	Next Run
Command-M	Minimize the frontmost window to the Dock
Shift-Z	Zoom Window

Reality Composer

▌ Version 1.4

Keyboard Shortcut	Action
Command-Comma	Open the preferences window
Command-H	Hide this app
Command-Option-H	Hide all other apps
Command-Q	Quit this app
Command-N	New
Command-O	Open
Command-W	Close the frontmost window
Command-S	Save the document
Command-Shift-S	Duplicate the document
Command-Shift-I	Import
Command-E	Export
Command-Z	Undo the previous command
Command-Shift-Z	Redo, revoking the undo command
Command-X	Cut the selected text or item and copy it to the clipboard
Command-C	Copy the selected text or item to the clipboard
Command-V	Paste the contents of the clipboard
Command-Option-V	Paste with Behaviors
Command-Option-Shift-V	Paste and Match Style
Command-D	Duplicate the selected item
Command-Shift-D	Duplicate with Behaviors
Delete	Delete
Command-A	Select all items

Keyboard Shortcut	Action
Return	Rename
Press Function Twice	Start voice dictation
Command-Control-Space Bar	Show the Character Viewer, which you can choose emoji and other symbols
Command-Option-T	Show Toolbar
Command-Control-S	Show Sidebar
Command-Control-F	Enter full screen
Command-M	Minimize the frontmost window to the Dock

Simulator

Version 11.5

Keyboard Shortcut	Action
Command-Comma	Open the preferences window
Command-H	Hide this app
Command-Option-H	Hide all other apps
Command-Q	Quit this app
Command-S	Save the screen
Command-W	Close the frontmost window
Command-Z	Undo the previous command
Command-Shift-Z	Redo, revoking the undo command
Command-Control-C	Copy screen
Command-Left Arrow	Rotate left
Command-Right Arrow	Rotate right
Command-Control-Z	Shake
Command-Shift-H	Home
Command-L	Lock
Command-Shift-B	Side Button
Command-Option-Shift-H	Siri
Command-Control-Shift-H	App Switcher
Command-Shift-K	Connect Hardware Keyboard
Command-K	Toggle Software Keyboard
Command-Shift-1	Shallow Press
Command-Shift-2	Deep Press
Command-Up Arrow	Increase Volume

Keyboard Shortcut	Action
Command-Down Arrow	Decrease Volume
Command-Option-M	Matching Touch (Touch ID)
Command-Shift-N	Non-matching Touch (Touch ID)
Command-Shift-A	Authorize Apple Pay
Command-Y	Toggle In-call Status Bar
Command-Shift-I	Trigger iCloud sync
Command-/	Open System Log
Command-Shift-M	Simulate Memory Warning
Command-M	Minimize the frontmost window to the Dock
Command-Shift-R	Show Apple TV Remote
Command-1	Physical Size
Command-2	Point Accurate
Command-3	Pixel Accurate

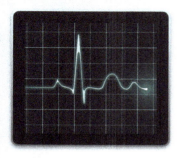

Activity Monitor

| Version 10.14

Keyboard Shortcut	Action
Command-H	Hide this app
Command-Option-H	Hide all other apps
Command-Q	Quit this app
Command-W	Close the frontmost window
Command-Shift-P	Show page setup for printing
Command-P	Print the document
Command-Z	Undo the previous command
Command-Shift-Z	Redo, revoking the undo command
Command-X	Cut the selected text or item and copy it to the clipboard
Command-C	Copy the selected text or item to the clipboard
Command-V	Paste the contents of the clipboard
Command-A	Select all items
Command-F	Find items in a document or app
Command-G	Find again: find the next occurrence of the item already found
Command-Shift-G	Find the previous occurrence
Command-E	Use Selection for Find
Command-J	Jump to selection
Command-Option-F	Filter Processes
Command-I	Inspect Process
Command-Option-S	Sample Process
Command-Option-Control-S	Run Spindump
Command-Option-Q	Quit Process

Keyboard Shortcut	Action
Command-Option-J	Show Deltas for Process
Command-K	Clear CPU History
Command-M	Minimize the frontmost window to the Dock
Command-1	Activity Monitor
Command-2	CPU Usage
Command-3	CPU History
Command-4	GPU History

Audio MIDI Setup

Version 3.5

Keyboard Shortcut	Action
Command-Comma	Open the preferences window
Command-H	Hide this app
Command-Option-H	Hide all other apps
Command-Q	Quit this app
Command-Z	Undo the previous command
Command-Shift-Z	Redo, revoking the undo command
Command-X	Cut the selected text or item and copy it to the clipboard
Command-C	Copy the selected text or item to the clipboard
Command-V	Paste the contents of the clipboard
Command-A	Select all items
Press Function Twice	Start voice dictation
Command-Control-Space Bar	Show the Character Viewer, which you can choose emoji and other symbols
Command-Option-T	Show Toolbar
Command-1	Hide Audio Devices
Command-2	Show MIDI Studio
Command-3	Show Network Device Browser
Command-W	Close the frontmost window
Command-M	Minimize the frontmost window to the Dock

Configurator 2

Version 2.12

Keyboard Shortcut	Action
Command-N	New Profile
Command-B	New Blueprint
Command-Option-N	New Window
Command-O	Open
Command-Shift-Backslash	Show All Tabs
Command-1	View as Collection
Command-2	View as List
Command-Forward Slash	Show Status Bar
Command-Option-T	Hide Toolbar
Command-R	Refresh
Control-Shift-Tab	Show Previous Tab
Control-Tab	Show Next Tab

Console

| Version 1.1

Keyboard Shortcut	Action
Command-N	New Profile
Command-B	New Blueprint
Command-Option-N	New Window
Command-O	Open
Command-Shift-Backslash	Show All Tabs
Command-1	View as Collection
Command-2	View as List
Command-Forward Slash	Show Status Bar
Command-Option-T	Hide Toolbar
Command-R	Refresh
Control-Shift-Tab	Show Previous Tab
Control-Tab	Show Next Tab

Digital Color Meter

| Version 5.15

Keyboard Shortcut	Action
Command-N	New Profile
Command-B	New Blueprint
Command-Option-N	New Window
Command-O	Open
Command-Shift-Backslash	Show All Tabs
Command-1	View as Collection
Command-2	View as List
Command-Forward Slash	Show Status Bar
Command-Option-T	Hide Toolbar
Command-R	Refresh
Control-Shift-Tab	Show Previous Tab
Control-Tab	Show Next Tab

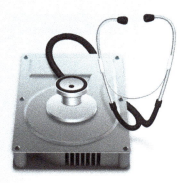

Disk Utility

Version 19.0

Keyboard Shortcut	Action
Command-H	Hide this app
Command-Option-H	Hide all other apps
Command-Q	Quit this app
Command-N	New Blank Image
Command-Shift-N	New Image from Folder
Command-Option-N	New Image from "Macintosh HD"
Command-Option-O	Open Disk Image
Command-W	Close the frontmost window
Command-I	Get Info
Command-E	Eject
Command-Shift-R	Restore
Command-Shift-P	Partition
Command-Shift-E	Erase
Command-Z	Undo the previous command
Command-Shift-Z	Redo, revoking the undo command
Command-X	Cut the selected text or item and copy it to the clipboard
Command-C	Copy the selected text or item to the clipboard
Command-V	Paste the contents of the clipboard
Command-A	Select all items
Command-F	Find items in a document or app
Command-Option-F	Find and Replace
Command-G	Find again: find the next occurrence of the item already found

Keyboard Shortcut	Action
Command-Shift-G	Find the previous occurrence
Command-J	Jump to selection
Command-Colon	Show spelling and grammar
Command-Semicolon	Check document now
Press Function Twice	Start voice dictation
Command-Control-Space Bar	Show the Character Viewer, which you can choose emoji and other symbols
Command-1	Show Only Volumes
Command-2	Show All Devices
Command-Option-3	Hide Sidebar
Command-Option-T	Hide Toolbar
Command-M	Minimize the frontmost window to the Dock
Command-D	Show Disk Utility Window

Keychain Access

Version 10.5

Keyboard Shortcut	Action
Command-Comma	Open the preferences window
Command-Option-K	Ticket Viewer
Command-H	Hide this app
Command-Option-H	Hide all other apps
Command-Q	Quit this app
Command-N	New Password Item
Command-Shift-N	New Secure Note Item
Command-Option-N	New Keychain
Command-Shift-I	Import Items
Command-Shift-E	Export Items
Command-Shift-A	Add Keychain
Command-Option-Delete	Delete Keychain Item
Command-W	Close the frontmost window
Command-I	Get Info
Command-L	Lock Keychain Item
Command-Z	Undo the previous command
Command-Shift-Z	Redo, revoking the undo command
Command-X	Cut the selected text or item and copy it to the clipboard
Command-C	Copy the selected text or item to the clipboard
Command-Shift-C	Copy Password to clipboard
Command-V	Paste the contents of the clipboard
Delete	Delete

Keyboard Shortcut	Action
Command-A	Select all items
Command-Option-F	Find
Press Function Twice	Start voice dictation
Command-Control-Space Bar	Show the Character Viewer, which you can choose emoji and other symbols
Command-K	Hide Keychains
Command-M	Minimize the frontmost window to the Dock
Command-1	Keychain Viewer

Script Editor

Version 2.11

Keyboard Shortcut	Action
Command-Comma	Open the preferences window
Command-H	Hide this app
Command-Option-H	Hide all other apps
Command-Q	Quit this app
Command-N	New
Command-O	Open
Command-Shift-O	Open Dictionary
Command-W	Close the frontmost window
Command-S	Save the document
Command-Shift-S	Duplicate the document
Command-Shift-P	Show page setup for printing
Command-P	Print the document
Command-0	Show Bundle Contents
Command-1	Show DEscapeription
Command-2	Show result
Command-3	Show log
Command-9	Show accessory view
Command-Z	Undo the previous command
Command-Shift-Z	Redo, revoking the undo command
Command-X	Cut the selected text or item and copy it to the clipboard
Command-C	Copy the selected text or item to the clipboard
Command-V	Paste the contents of the clipboard

Keyboard Shortcut	Action
Command-Option-Shift-V	Paste and Match Style
Command-Shift-V	Paste Reference
Command-A	Select all items
Option-Escape	Complete
Press Function Twice	Start voice dictation
Command-F	Find items in a document or app
Command-G	Find again: find the next occurrence of the item already found
Command-Shift-G	Find the previous occurrence
Command-Shift-F	Hide find bar
Command-E	Use Selection for Find
Command-J	Jump to selection
Command-Control-Space Bar	Show the Character Viewer, which you can choose emoji and other symbols
Command-Shift-R	Record
Command-Period	Stop
Command-R	Run
Command-Option-R	Run App
Command-K	Compile
Command-T	Show Fonts
Command-B	Bold
Command-I	Italic
Command-U	Underline
Command-Plus	Bigger
Command-Minus	Smaller
Command-Shift-C	Show Colors
Command-Option-C	Copy style
Command-Option-V	Paste Style
Command-Right Curly Bracket	Align Right
Command-Vertical Bar	Center
Command-Right Curly Bracket	Align Right
Command-Control-C	Copy ruler
Command-Control-V	Paste Ruler

Keyboard Shortcut	Action
Command-M	Minimize the frontmost window to the Dock
Command-Option-L	Log History
Command-Shift-L	Library

Terminal

Version 2.10

Keyboard Shortcut	Action
Command-Comma	Open the preferences window
Command-H	Hide this app
Command-Option-H	Hide all other apps
Command-Q	Quit this app
Command-N	New Window with Profile
Command-Control-N	New Window with Same Command
Command-T	New Tab with Profile
Command-Control-T	New Tab with Same Command
Command-Shift-N	New Command
Command-Shift-K	New Remote Connection
Command-O	Import
Command-W	Close the frontmost window
Command-S	Export Text As
Command-Shift-S	Export Selected Text As
Command-I	Show Inspector
Command-Shift-I	Edit Title
Command-Option-I	Edit Background Color
Command-Option-R	Reset
Command-Option-Control-R	Hard Reset
Command-Option-P	Print Selection
Command-P	Print the document
Command-Z	Undo the previous command

Keyboard Shortcut	Action
Command-Shift-Z	Redo, revoking the undo command
Command-X	Cut the selected text or item and copy it to the clipboard
Command-Control-Shift-C	Copy without background color
Command-Option-Shift-C	Copy Plain Text
Command-V	Paste the contents of the clipboard
Command-Control-V	Paste Escaped Text
Command-Shift-V	Paste Selection
Command-A	Select all items
Command-Shift-A	Select Between Marks
Command-Return	Mark Line and Send Return
Command-Shift-Return	Send Return Without Marking
Command-U	Mark
Command-Option-U	Mark as Bookmark
Command-Shift-U	Unmark
Command-Shift-M	Insert Bookmark
Command-Option-Shift-M	Insert Bookmark with Name
Command-Shift-Arrow Up	Select to Previous Mark
Command-Shift-Down Arrow	Select to Next Mark
Command-Option-Shift-Up Arrow	Select to Previous Bookmark
Command-Option-Shift-Arrow Down	Select to Next Bookmark
Command-L	Clear to Previous Mark
Command-Option-L	Clear to Previous Bookmark
Command-K	Clear to start
Command-Option-K	Clear scrollback
Command-Control-L	Clear screen
Command-F	Find items in a document or app
Command-G	Find again: find the next occurrence of the item already found
Command-Shift-G	Find the previous occurrence
Command-Shift-F	Hide Find Bar
Command-E	Use selection for find
Command-J	Jump to Selection

Keyboard Shortcut	Action
Command-Shift-C	Show Colors
Command-Option-O	Use Option as Meta Key
Press Function Twice	Start voice dictation
Command-Control-Space Bar	Show the Character Viewer, which you can choose emoji and other symbols
Command-Shift-Backslash	Show All Tabs
Command-Shift-T	Show Tab Bar
Command-Page Down	Show Alternate Screen
Command-Shift-Page Up	Hide Alternate Screen
Command-R	Allow Mouse Reporting
Command-D	Split Pane
Command-Shift-D	Close Split Pane
Command-0	Default Font Size
Command-Plus Sign	Bigger
Command-Minus Sign	Smaller
Command-Home	Scroll to Top
Command-End	Scroll to Bottom
Command-Page Up	Page Up
Command-Page Down	Page Down
Command-Option-Page Up	Line Up
Command-Option-Page Down	Line Down
Command-Control-F	Enter full screen
Command-M	Minimize the frontmost window to the Dock
Command-Grave Accent	Cycle through windows
Control-Shift-Tab	Show Previous Tab
Control-Tab	Show Next Tab
Command-Control-Question Mark	Open man page for item
Command-Option-Control-Forward Slash	Search man page index for item

VoiceOver Utility

Version 10

Keyboard Shortcut	Action
Command-H	Hide this app
Command-Option-H	Hide all other apps
Command-Q	Quit this app
Command-Shift-I	Import Preferences
Command-Shift-E	Export Preferences
Command-Shift-V	Set Up Portable Preferences
Command-Z	Undo the previous command
Command-Shift-Z	Redo, revoking the undo command
Command-X	Cut the selected text or item and copy it to the clipboard
Command-C	Copy the selected text or item to the clipboard
Command-V	Paste the contents of the clipboard
Command-A	Select all items
Command-D	Duplicate the selected item
Command-N	New Entry
Command-Up Arrow	Move up
Command-Down Arrow	Move down
Command-B	Memorize Braille Key
Command-F	Find items in a document or app
Command-Colon	Show Spelling and grammar
Command-Semicolon	Check spelling
Press Function Twice	Start voice dictation
Command-Control-Space Bar	Show the Character Viewer, which you can choose emoji and other symbols

Keyboard Shortcut	Action
Command-1	General
Command-2	Verbosity
Command-3	Speech
Command-4	Navigation
Command-5	Web
Command-6	Sound
Command-7	Visuals
Command-8	Commanders
Command-9	Braille
Command-0	Activities
Command-W	Close the frontmost window
Command-M	Minimize the frontmost window to the Dock

About the Author

Jordan Kennedy has been a Macintosh and technology enthuasist for more than fifteen years. A designer by trade, Jordan has over a decade of professional experience in graphic design, UX design, and web development.

Jordan lives with his husband and their sweet cat, Lucky, in Murfreesboro, Tennessee.

You can reach Jordan by visiting his website at jordankennedy.com or via Twitter @jryankennedy.

www.ingramcontent.com/pod-product-compliance
Lightning Source LLC
Chambersburg PA
CBHW080551060326
40689CB00021B/4817